Practical C++ Machine Learning

Hands-on strategies for developing simple machine learning models using C++ data structures and libraries

Anais Sutherland

Published by: GitforGits

Publisher: Sonal Dhandre

www.gitforgits.com

support@gitforgits.com

Printed in India

First Printing: November 2024

ISBN: 978-81-979504-8-3

Cover Design by: Kitten Publishing

Prologue

When I first started out in the field of machine learning, I was blown away by the vast number of tools and libraries that were available for programming languages such as Python. On the other hand, as a dedicated C++ programmer, I was confronted with the challenge of locating resources that were tailored to my preferred programming language. Despite the fact that C++ is unrivaled in terms of its power and efficiency, the incorporation of machine learning into C++ projects appeared to be a challenging endeavor due to the absence of any practical guidance.

I remember spending countless hours trying to bridge the gap between the concepts of machine learning and their implementation in C++. I did this by piecing together information from a variety of sources. The difficulties were numerous, including the establishment of the appropriate environment, the discovery of appropriate libraries, and the modification of algorithms that are typically demonstrated in other languages. I came to the realization that there must be other people who share my passion for C++ and are eager to take advantage of the possibilities offered by machine learning without having to switch to a different programming language.

As a result of that journey, this book was released. I wanted to develop a resource that is geared specifically toward C++ developers and offers them the opportunity to gain hands-on, practical experience in the process of constructing machine learning models. It was my intention to remove some of the mystery behind the process by demonstrating that not only is it feasible, but it is also gratifying to implement and deploy machine learning solutions using C++. My goal is to equip other programmers with the confidence to confidently incorporate machine learning into their C++ projects by guiding them through real-world examples and addressing common challenges head-on.

Over the course of the chapters, I have sought to disseminate not only code, but also insights and lessons that I have gained from my own experiences. Each and every section is designed to impart practical abilities that can be utilized right away, beginning with the configuration of the development environment and ending with the optimization of models for performance performance. To the best of my knowledge, it is possible to fully exploit the capabilities of C++ in order to develop machine learning applications that are both high-performing and efficient.

-- Anais Sutherland

Content

Preface

Practical C++ Machine Learning introduces C++ programmers to the world of machine learning. If you know C++ but haven't worked with machine learning solutions before, this book is a good place to start learning the basics and experimenting with the language's essential concepts and techniques.

The book starts off by showing you how to set up a development environment and put together some basic neural networks using the Flashlight library. It then covers essential tasks like data preprocessing, model training, and evaluation, with practical examples that show how machine learning works in a C++ context. You will also learn strategies for dealing with common problems like overfitting and performance optimization. The next few chapters get into more complex topics like convolutional neural networks, model deployment, and some key performance tuning techniques. This will help you develop and integrate your own models into applications.

By the end of the book, you will have essential hands-on experience and a better clarity to explore and expand your machine learning knowledge in C++. This book doesn't aim to cover everything, but it does serve as a good starting point for you to confidently dive into the world of machine learning and deep learning.

In this book you will learn to:

- Use Flashlight to set up a C++ environment for machine learning projects.
- Implement neural networks from scratch to gain a hands-on understanding.
- Preprocess and augment data effectively to improve model performance.
- Train and evaluate models using appropriate loss functions and metrics.
- Explore overfitting challenges with techniques like regularization and dropout.
- Build advanced architectures like ResNet.
- Apply transfer learning to leverage pre-trained models.
- Deploy models and integrate them into real-world C++ apps.
- Implement real-time inference with optimized performance.
- Improve performance using GPU acceleration and multi-threading techniques.

GitforGits

Prerequisites

For those interested in learning the fundamentals of machine learning and how to apply them to the development of systems, applications, games, and hardware, this book is a great resource. It is suitable for both novice and seasoned C++ programmers.

Codes Usage

Are you in need of some helpful code examples to assist you in your programming and documentation? Look no further! Our book offers a wealth of supplemental material, including code examples and exercises.

Not only is this book here to aid you in getting your job done, but you have our permission to use the example code in your programs and documentation. However, please note that if you are reproducing a significant portion of the code, we do require you to contact us for permission.

But don't worry, using several chunks of code from this book in your program or answering a question by citing our book and quoting example code does not require permission. But if you do choose to give credit, an attribution typically includes the title, author, publisher, and ISBN. For example, "Practical C++ Machine Learning by Anais Sutherland".

If you are unsure whether your intended use of the code examples falls under fair use or the permissions outlined above, please do not hesitate to reach out to us at support@gitforgits.com.

We are happy to assist and clarify any concerns.

Acknowledgement

I owe a tremendous debt of gratitude to GitforGits, for their unflagging enthusiasm and wise counsel throughout the entire process of writing this book. Their knowledge and careful editing helped make sure the piece was useful for people of all reading levels and comprehension skills. In addition, I'd like to thank everyone involved in the publishing process for their efforts in making this book a reality. Their efforts, from copyediting to advertising, made the project what it is today.

Finally, I'd like to express my gratitude to everyone who has shown me unconditional love and encouragement throughout my life. Their support was crucial to the completion of this book. I appreciate your help with this endeavour and your continued interest in my career.

CHAPTER 1: GETTING STARTED WITH C++ MACHINE LEARNING

Chapter Overview

Welcome to the first chapter of "Practical C++ Machine Learning." We're going to dive into the fascinating world of combining the strong abilities of C++ with the fast-changing field of machine learning. We will start by looking at the key moments and developments in machine learning, giving you a quick overview of why it's so important in today's tech world. Then, we will look at how C++ can help with machine learning. We will see how it can be used to create high-performance ML applications thanks to its performance efficiency and control over system resources.

We will introduce you to the CIFAR-10 dataset, which is a widely used image dataset that we will use as our primary example throughout the book. This will help you grasp the practical aspects of implementing ML models. Next, we will set up your development environment. We will show you how to install the necessary tools and the Flashlight library, so You will be ready to start coding without any problems. And then, we will bring it all together by writing your first C++ machine learning program, giving you hands-on experience to set the stage for more complex projects ahead. Once You are done with this chapter, You will have a solid starting point and be ready to dive into the nitty-gritty of machine learning.

Highlights of Machine Learning

In the past few years, machine learning has changed a lot. It went from being a theoretical field of study to being used in many areas of our daily lives very quickly. The availability of huge amounts of data and the rise in computing power have put machine learning at the forefront of technological progress. A lot of smart systems, like Siri and Alexa, use machine learning algorithms to make decisions. Netflix and Amazon also use them to make suggestions. They learn from data, find patterns, and make decisions with little help from humans. This makes them very useful for solving hard problems in many fields and opens up a huge number of opportunities for programmers and developers. Machine learning makes it possible to make more complex apps that can look at data, guess what will happen, and make the user experience better. Developers who are good at machine learning can work on cutting edge projects in areas like autonomous vehicles. Algorithms let cars drive safely on the roads by reading traffic signs and guessing where people will walk. Machine learning models help doctors figure out what diseases people have by looking at medical images and patient data more accurately than old ways of doing things. Financial institutions use machine learning to spot fraudulent transactions by noticing strange patterns in how people spend their money. This makes users safer.

The growth of machine learning has also led to the creation of new programming languages and tools, which push programmers to learn new things. When developers understand the basics of machine learning, they can make apps that can change and learn over time, making services more personalized and effective. In natural language processing, for example, machine learning helps chatbots understand and answer user questions in a more natural way, which makes customer service better. Businesses are relying more and more on data-driven decisions, so programmers who are good at machine learning are in high demand to make models that can look at trends and predict what will happen in the future. There are a lot of different ways that machine learning techniques can be used. Face recognition is done with machine learning algorithms in computer vision. This lets security systems figure out who someone is and let them in based on that information. Machine learning is used by social media sites to find and remove inappropriate content, keeping the internet safer. In environmental science, machine learning models help predict climate change by looking at weather patterns. This makes it easier to be ready for disasters and manage resources. Machine learning helps farmers get the most out of their crops by looking at data about the soil, the weather, and the health of the plants. This leads to more sustainable farming methods.

Machine learning makes the entertainment industry more interesting by suggesting music, movies, and books based on what each person likes. Streaming services look at what users watch to suggest content that fits their tastes. This keeps users on the platform longer. In sports, teams use machine learning to look at data about how players are doing and come up with strategies that can help them win. Language translation services also use machine learning to make translations more accurate and aware of the context, which makes it easier for people all over the world to communicate. Machine learning is also making big steps forward in the field of education. Personalized learning platforms give each student the resources and exercises that work best for them based on their learning style and speed. This helps students learn better and can help close gaps in their education. In cybersecurity, machine learning algorithms find threats and act on them right away, finding holes in security before they can be used. These systems can fix security problems before they happen by looking at network traffic and user behavior. This keeps sensitive data and infrastructure safe. As machine learning improves, it also helps robotics come up with new ideas. Algorithms make it possible for robots to do everything from simple housework to complicated factory work. Machine learning improves manufacturing by figuring out when equipment will break down and planning maintenance, which cuts down on downtime and boosts efficiency. By looking at genetic data to understand diseases at the molecular level, machine learning helps the field of genomics. This makes personalized medicine possible.

Machine learning is making fast progress not only in making systems smarter, but also in giving programmers and developers the tools they need to make solutions that can have a big effect on society. Processing and learning from data makes it possible to create apps that can solve some of the world's most important problems. Because we are creating more data than ever before, machine learning is becoming more and more important for understanding and using it. Learning the ideas and methods behind machine learning gives programmers the chance to be on the cutting edge of new technology, which drives progress in many fields and industries.

Potential of C++ in ML

When it comes to machine learning, Python often steals the spotlight due to its simplicity and the vast ecosystem of libraries. However, C++ holds significant potential in the machine learning landscape, especially when performance and efficiency are paramount. C++ offers fine-grained control over system resources, allowing developers to optimize algorithms for speed and memory usage. This control is crucial in scenarios where processing large datasets or running complex models requires maximum computational efficiency, such as real-time systems or applications deployed on resource-constrained devices.

One of the positive aspects of using C++ for machine learning is its ability to execute code at blazing speeds. C++ compiles down to machine code, which runs directly on the hardware, eliminating the overhead associated with interpreted languages. This makes C++ an excellent choice for performance-critical applications like high-frequency trading systems, where milliseconds can make a significant difference. C++ also supports concurrent and parallel programming paradigms, enabling developers to fully utilize multi-core processors and GPUs for training and running machine learning models, thereby reducing execution time significantly. The language's maturity and stability are also advantages. C++ has been around for decades and has undergone numerous improvements, resulting in a robust language with a rich set of features. Its compatibility with legacy systems allows for seamless integration of machine learning capabilities into existing C++ applications without the need to rewrite code in another language. This interoperability is valuable for organizations looking to enhance their software with machine learning features while maintaining their existing codebase.

Several high-quality machine learning libraries are available in C++, providing developers with tools to implement complex models efficiently. **Flashlight** is one such library, designed for flexibility and performance. It's a deep learning library that emphasizes efficiency and scalability, making it suitable for both research and production environments. Flashlight provides a modular approach, allowing developers to build custom models by combining different components. Its support for GPU acceleration enables handling large-scale machine learning tasks effectively.

PaddlePaddle (PArallel Distributed Deep LEarning), developed by Baidu, is another powerful C++ library. It's designed to be easy to use and highly efficient, supporting a wide range of neural network architectures and machine learning tasks. PaddlePaddle's design focuses on parallelism and distribution, allowing models to be trained across multiple machines and GPUs, which is essential for big data applications. Its rich feature set and active community support make it a valuable tool for developers working on complex machine learning projects.

LightGBM is a gradient boosting framework that uses tree-based learning algorithms, known for its speed and efficiency. Developed by Microsoft, LightGBM is particularly effective for ranking, classification, and many other machine learning tasks. Its implementation allows it to leverage low-level optimizations, making it faster and more memory-efficient compared to other gradient boosting libraries. LightGBM supports parallel learning, GPU acceleration, and can handle large-scale data, making it suitable for production environments where performance is critical.

Real-world machine learning applications built upon C++ demonstrate the language's capabilities in handling demanding tasks. For instance, many high-frequency trading platforms use C++ for implementing machine learning algorithms that analyze market data and make trading decisions in real-time. The need for ultra-low latency and high throughput in these systems makes C++ the ideal choice. Autonomous vehicles also rely on machine learning algorithms written in C++ to process sensor data and make split-second decisions. The performance and reliability of C++ are essential in ensuring the safety and efficiency of these vehicles. In the field of computer vision, applications like OpenCV are predominantly written in C++ due to the necessity for high-performance image and video processing. Machine learning models integrated into these applications can perform tasks such as object detection, facial recognition, and motion tracking with minimal latency. These capabilities are crucial in areas like surveillance, augmented reality, and robotics, where real-time processing is non-negotiable. Moreover, large tech companies often use C++ for their backend systems that require machine learning capabilities. For example, search engines might implement ranking algorithms and spam detection to handle the massive scale of data and requests efficiently. The robustness and speed of C++ ensure that these systems can provide quick and accurate results to users around the globe.

In embedded systems and IoT devices, where resources are limited, C++ shines by allowing developers to write efficient code that can run machine learning models locally. This is important for applications like smart home devices, wearable technology, and industrial sensors, where sending data to the cloud for processing isn't feasible due to latency or privacy concerns. By utilizing C++, developers can optimize these applications to perform machine learning tasks on-device, providing faster responses and enhanced user experiences. The gaming industry also benefits from machine learning models implemented in C++. Game engines often use C++ for its performance advantages, and integrating machine learning can enhance AI behavior, procedural content generation, and player analytics. This integration can lead to more immersive and responsive gaming experiences. As machine learning continues to expand into new domains, the role of C++ is poised to grow, offering developers a powerful platform to create innovative and efficient solutions.

Introduction to the CIFAR-10 Dataset

What is CIFAR-10 Dataset?

The CIFAR-10 dataset is a widely recognized benchmark in the field of machine learning and computer vision. It consists of 60,000 color images, each with a resolution of 32x32 pixels. These images are categorized into 10 distinct classes, with 6,000 images per class. The classes represent everyday objects and animals: airplanes, automobiles, birds, cats, deer, dogs, frogs, horses, ships, and trucks. This diversity makes the dataset an excellent tool for training and evaluating image classification algorithms. The dataset is publicly available and can be downloaded from the official website: https://www.cs.toronto.edu/~kriz/cifar.html.

CIFAR-10 is an ideal choice for this book because it strikes a balance between complexity and manageability. The dataset is challenging enough to demonstrate the practical aspects of machine learning algorithms, yet it's small enough to be handled without requiring massive computational resources. This makes it accessible for those who may not have access to high-end hardware but still want to gain hands-on experience. By working with CIFAR-10, You will be able to apply various machine learning techniques and observe their effects on real-world data, providing a solid foundation for understanding more complex datasets in the future.

Throughout this book, we will use the CIFAR-10 dataset as a consistent example to teach different machine learning algorithms and techniques. Starting from basic data handling and preprocessing, we will walk through you the steps necessary to prepare the dataset for training models. This includes normalizing the images, converting them into appropriate data structures, and splitting the dataset into training and testing sets. By working with actual data, You will gain a deeper understanding of the importance of these preprocessing steps and how they impact model performance.

Applying Algorithms and Techniques with CIFAR-10

As we progress, we will implement various machine learning models, starting with simple neural networks and advancing to more complex architectures like convolutional neural networks (CNNs) and deep residual networks. You will learn how to build, train, and evaluate these models using C++ and the Flashlight library using CIFAR-10 as your test case. Each chapter will introduce new techniques, such as data augmentation, regularization, and hyperparameter tuning, all applied to the CIFAR-10 dataset. You can build your knowledge incrementally without the distraction of adapting to new datasets or domains because this continuity allows you to do so. You will be able to directly compare the outcomes of different models and techniques since they are all applied to the same data. This approach reveals the strengths and weaknesses of each method, enabling you to make informed decisions when choosing algorithms for your own projects.

You will have the skills needed to tackle real-world machine learning problems by working extensively with CIFAR-10. You will encounter these challenges in many applications: handling image data, dealing with class imbalances, and optimizing model performance. You will be better prepared to apply your knowledge to more complex datasets and tasks in fields like medical imaging, autonomous driving, or surveillance systems by overcoming these challenges in a controlled environment.

Integration with C++ and Flashlight

Using C++ in conjunction with the Flashlight library to work with CIFAR-10 provides a unique opportunity to understand the intricacies of machine learning implementation at a deeper level. You will gain insight into how data is managed in memory, how computations are performed efficiently, and how to optimize code for better performance. Throughout the book, we will include hands-on exercises and mini-projects centered around the CIFAR-10 dataset. These activities are designed to reinforce the concepts discussed in each chapter and provide practical experience. For example, after learning about CNNs, you might be tasked with improving a model's accuracy by experimenting with different architectures or hyperparameters. These exercises not only solidify your understanding but also encourage experimentation and critical thinking.

While CIFAR-10 is the primary dataset used in this book, the skills and knowledge you gain are transferable to other datasets and domains. The principles of data preprocessing, model building, training, and evaluation remain consistent across different types of data. You will be well-equipped to take on more complex challenges, whether that's working with larger images, different data modalities, or implementing state-of-the-art architectures.

Setting up the Development Environment

Before we begin, make sure you have administrative privileges on your Linux machine, as some installations require **sudo** access. We will be using Ubuntu, but the steps are similar for other Linux distributions.

Install C++ Compiler

First, you need a modern C++ compiler that supports C++17 or later. The GNU Compiler Collection (GCC) is a popular choice.

First, open a terminal and update your package lists to ensure you have the latest information:

```
sudo apt update
```

Install the essential compilation tools, including GCC and G++:

```
sudo apt install build-essential
```

Check the installed version to confirm:

```
g++ --version
```

You should see output similar to:

```
g++ (Ubuntu 9.3.0-17ubuntu1~20.04) 9.3.0
```

Here, ensure that the version is at least 7.0 to support C++17 features.

Install CMake

CMake is a cross-platform tool that simplifies the build process for C++ projects. To do this, use the following command:

```
sudo apt install cmake
```

Check the version:

```
cmake --version
```

Output should be:

```
cmake version 3.16.3
```

And finally, you have to make sure the version is 3.10 or higher.

Installing Dependencies

We all know that Flashlight relies on several libraries and they need to be within the working environment. So, we will install them as follows:

Install OpenBLAS

OpenBLAS is an optimized BLAS library:

```
sudo apt install libopenblas-dev
```

Install FFTW

FFTW is a C library for computing the discrete Fourier transform:

```
sudo apt install libfftw3-dev
```

Install Other Dependencies

Install additional required libraries:

```
sudo apt install libeigen3-dev
sudo apt install libgflags-dev libgoogle-glog-dev libgtest-dev
sudo apt install libspdlog-dev
```

In addition, Flashlight uses ArrayFire for tensor operations. So, first add the ArrayFire PPA:

```
sudo add-apt-repository ppa:arrayfire/ppa
sudo apt update
```

Then, install ArrayFire as below:

```
sudo apt install arrayfire-dev
```

Now, we will download and install Flashlight from its GitHub repository. For this, we will navigate to your development directory and clone the repo:

```
git clone https://github.com/flashlight/flashlight.git
```

Thrn, we create a build directory:

```
cd flashlight
mkdir build && cd build
```

We then configure the Build with Cmake.

```
cmake .. -DCMAKE_BUILD_TYPE=Release -DFLASHLIGHT_BACKEND=CPU
```

If you have an NVIDIA GPU and CUDA installed, you can enable GPU support:

```
cmake .. -DCMAKE_BUILD_TYPE=Release -DFLASHLIGHT_BACKEND=CUDA
```

Compile Flashlight

Next, we use **make** to build the library:

```
make -j$(nproc)
```

The **-j$(nproc)** flag tells **make** to use all available processor cores, speeding up the build process.

Install the library system-wide:

```
sudo make install
```

With this, we are then installing Flashlight headers and libraries to **/usr/local/include** and **/usr/local/lib** respectively.

Setting Environment Variables

To ensure your system can locate the Flashlight libraries, update your environment variables, primarily **LD_LIBRARY_PATH.**

Here, we first add the following line to your **~/.bashrc** or **~/.bash_profile**:

```
export LD_LIBRARY_PATH=/usr/local/lib:$LD_LIBRARY_PATH
```

Next, source the updated file:

```
source ~/.bashrc
```

Now, we will now write a simple program to test the installation.

Create a Test Program

Create a file named **test_flashlight.cpp**:

```
#include <flashlight/flashlight.h>
#include <iostream>
int main() {
    // Create a 2x2 tensor filled with ones
    fl::Tensor tensor = fl::full({2, 2}, 1.0);
    // Perform an operation
    tensor = tensor + 5;
    // Print the result
    std::cout << "Tensor:\n" << tensor << std::endl;
    return 0;
}
```

Next, compile using the following command:

```
g++ test_flashlight.cpp -lflashlight -larrayfire -o
test_flashlight
```

If you installed Flashlight in a custom directory, you might need to specify include and library paths:

```
g++ test_flashlight.cpp -I/usr/local/include -L/usr/local/lib
-lflashlight -larrayfire -o test_flashlight
```

Then execute the compiled program:

```
./test_flashlight
```

Following can be the expected output which is fine to us:

```
Tensor:
[2 2 1 1]
    6.0000      6.0000
```

```
    6.0000    6.0000
```

This confirms that Flashlight is correctly installed and functional.

Download CIFAR-10 Dataset

We will be using the CIFAR-10 dataset in our projects. In your project root, first create a **data** directory:

```
mkdir -p ~/ml_project/data
cd ~/ml_project/data
```

Use **wget** to download and then extract:

```
wget https://www.cs.toronto.edu/~kriz/cifar-10-binary.tar.gz
tar -xvzf cifar-10-binary.tar.gz
```

The dataset is now available in the **cifar-10-batches-bin** directory.

Setting up Project Structure and Running Project

- Create Directories

```
mkdir -p ~/ml_project/src
mkdir -p ~/ml_project/include
mkdir -p ~/ml_project/build
```

- Create a CMakeLists.txt File

In your project root (**~/ml_project**), create a **CMakeLists.txt** file:

```
cmake_minimum_required(VERSION 3.10)
project(MLProject)
set(CMAKE_CXX_STANDARD 17)
find_package(flashlight REQUIRED)
include_directories(${FLASHLIGHT_INCLUDE_DIRS})
link_directories(${FLASHLIGHT_LIBRARY_DIRS})
add_executable(ml_project src/main.cpp)
```

```
target_link_libraries(ml_project flashlight)
```

- Navigate to the Build Directory

```
cd ~/ml_project/build
```

- Run CMake

```
cmake ..
```

- Compile the Project

```
make
```

- Run the Executable

```
./ml_project
```

If you encounter errors about missing headers, ensure the paths you included are correct in the **CMakeLists.txt**. And for linker errors, try to verify that the library paths are correctly specified.

Introduction to Flashlight

Flashlight is an open-source, flexible machine learning library written entirely in C++. It is designed to facilitate research and development of machine learning algorithms, focusing on performance and modularity. Flashlight leverages the ArrayFire tensor library for high-performance computing, allowing you to run your models on CPUs, GPUs, or other accelerators without changing your code.

Key Features of Flashlight

- The flashlight is designed with performance in mind. It uses ArrayFire to handle tensor operations, which means the code is optimized for whatever hardware You are working with, whether it's a CPU or GPU.
- The library is designed with a modular architecture, so it's easy to add different components like layers, loss functions, and optimizers. You can try out lots of different neural network structures with this design pretty quickly.
- As a pure C++ library, Flashlight lets you integrate it seamlessly with your existing C++ codebases. This is really helpful for projects where you need to be sure your performance is up there and you have full control over the low-level stuff.

- Flashlight gets rid of the need to worry about the hardware You are using, so you can run your code on different devices with no hassle. You've got the option of using a CPU, CUDA for NVIDIA GPUs, or OpenCL backends.

Just to let you know, the project is kept up to date with new developments thanks to a very active and engaged community, who provide support and input.

Why Flashlight for this Book?

Flashlight is chosen for this book because it aligns perfectly with our goal of teaching practical machine learning using C++. Following are certain aspects that puts higher preference for Flashlight over other libraries:

- Flashlight's design exposes you to the inner workings of machine learning models. Unlike higher-level frameworks that abstract away details, Flashlight allows you to understand what's happening under the hood.
- By using C++ and optimizing for performance, Flashlight enables you to work with computationally intensive models efficiently. This is critical when scaling up to larger datasets or more complex architectures.
- For developers already familiar with C++, Flashlight provides a natural extension into machine learning without the need to switch languages or deal with language bindings.
- Flashlight supports a wide range of machine learning tasks, from basic neural networks to advanced models, making it a suitable tool throughout this book as we explore different concepts.

Core Components of Flashlight

Tensor Operations

The **fl::Tensor** class is at the heart of Flashlight, representing multi-dimensional arrays. It supports a variety of operations like slicing, indexing, mathematical computations, and more.

```
// Creating a tensor
fl::Tensor tensor = fl::rand({3, 3});
// Performing an operation
fl::Tensor result = fl::sin(tensor);
```

Neural Network Modules

Flashlight provides modules for building neural networks, such as linear layers, convolutional layers, activation functions, and pooling layers.

```
// Defining a linear layer
auto linear = std::make_shared<fl::Linear>(input_size,
output_size);
// Using the layer
fl::Tensor output = linear->forward(input_tensor);
```

Loss Functions

Loss functions measure how well your model is performing. Flashlight includes common losses like Mean Squared Error and Cross-Entropy Loss.

```
// Cross-Entropy Loss
fl::CategoricalCrossEntropy loss_fn;
// Calculating loss
fl::Tensor loss = loss_fn(output, target);
```

Optimizers

Optimizers adjust the model's parameters to minimize the loss function. Flashlight supports optimizers like Stochastic Gradient Descent (SGD) and Adam.

```
// Creating an optimizer
fl::SGDOptimizer optimizer(model_params, learning_rate);
// Updating parameters
optimizer.step();
```

Building a Simple Model using Flashlight

To illustrate how Flashlight works, we will build a simple neural network model with following steps:

- Define the Model

```
class SimpleNN : public fl::Container {
public:
    SimpleNN(int input_size, int hidden_size, int output_size)
{
```

```
        add(fl::Linear(input_size, hidden_size));
        add(fl::ReLU());
        add(fl::Linear(hidden_size, output_size));
    }
    fl::Variable forward(const fl::Variable& input) override {
        return Container::forward(input);
    }
};
```

- Initialize the Model

```
int input_size = 784;  // For example, MNIST images flattened
int hidden_size = 128;
int output_size = 10;  // Number of classes
auto model = std::make_shared<SimpleNN>(input_size,
hidden_size, output_size);
```

- Setup the Training Loop

```
fl::SGDOptimizer optimizer(model->params(), 0.01);
fl::CategoricalCrossEntropy loss_fn;
for (int epoch = 0; epoch < num_epochs; ++epoch) {
    for (auto& batch : data_loader) {
        fl::Tensor inputs = batch.inputs;
        fl::Tensor targets = batch.targets;
        // Forward pass
        fl::Variable outputs = model-
>forward(fl::Variable(inputs, false));
        // Compute loss
        fl::Variable loss = loss_fn(outputs,
fl::Variable(targets, false));
        // Backward pass
        optimizer.zeroGrad();
```

```
        loss.backward();
        // Update parameters
        optimizer.step();
    }
}
```

This example shows you how to put together a basic neural network, set up a loss function, and get a training loop up and running using Flashlight. The more machine learning develops, the more valuable it'll be to have expertise in efficient, low-level implementations.

Writing your First C++ ML Program

Now that our development environment is ready, familiarized ourselves with the Flashlight library and also built a simple model using it, it's time to write our first a decent machine learning program. Or we can simply create a simple "Hello World" program that utilizes Flashlight to perform a basic machine learning task.

Creating Project Structure and Writing Code

First, we will set up the basic structure for our program. Open the terminal and navigate to your project's source directory. Then, we will create a file named **main.cpp** where we will write our code:

```
cd ~/ml_project/src
touch main.cpp
```

Next, open **main.cpp** in your favorite text editor and start coding. Here, first begin by including the essential headers from the Flashlight library and the standard input-output stream:

```
#include <flashlight/flashlight.h>
#include <iostream>
```

Next, set up the main function where our program will execute:

```
int main() {
    // Our code will go here
    return 0;
```

```
}
```

After this, since we haven't covered loading the actual CIFAR-10 dataset yet, we will simulate input data using random tensors:

```
int batchSize = 4;
int numClasses = 10; // CIFAR-10 has 10 classes
// Create a random input tensor representing images
fl::Tensor input = fl::rand({32, 32, 3, batchSize}); //
Dimensions: 32x32 pixels, 3 color channels, batch size
// Create random target labels
fl::Tensor target = fl::randint({batchSize}, fl::dtype::s32) %
numClasses;
```

Then, we will construct a basic neural network model with one linear layer:

```
// Flatten the input tensor from 3D to 1D
auto flatten = std::make_shared<fl::View>({-1, batchSize});
// Create a linear layer
auto linear = std::make_shared<fl::Linear>(32 * 32 * 3,
numClasses);
// Combine layers into a sequential model
auto model = fl::Sequential();
model.add(flatten);
model.add(linear);
```

After this, we will use the categorical cross-entropy loss function and stochastic gradient descent (SGD) optimizer:

```
// Define the loss function
auto criterion = fl::CategoricalCrossEntropy();
// Set up the optimizer
fl::SGDOptimizer optimizer(model.params(), 0.01); // Learning
rate of 0.01
```

Now, continue to pass the input data through the model to get predictions:

```
// Convert input to a variable and disable gradient
computation
fl::Variable inputVar(input, false);
// Forward pass to get model output
fl::Variable output = model.forward(inputVar);
```

After this, simply calculate the loss between the model's output and the target labels:

```
// Convert target to a variable
fl::Variable targetVar(target, false);
// Compute the loss
fl::Variable loss = criterion(output, targetVar);
```

We shall then perform backpropagation and update the model's parameters:

```
// Zero the gradients
optimizer.zeroGrad();
// Backward pass to compute gradients
loss.backward();
// Update the parameters
optimizer.step();
```

After this, it is good to output the loss value to the console:

```
// Print the loss
std::cout << "Loss: " << loss.scalar<float>() << std::endl;P
```

Program Compiling and Running

Now, we will compile and run our program to ensure everything works as expected. To do this, we first ensure the **CMakeLists.txt** includes the necessary configurations:

```
cmake_minimum_required(VERSION 3.10)
project(MLProject)
set(CMAKE_CXX_STANDARD 17)
find_package(flashlight REQUIRED)
```

```
include_directories(${FLASHLIGHT_INCLUDE_DIRS})
link_directories(${FLASHLIGHT_LIBRARY_DIRS})
add_executable(ml_project src/main.cpp)
target_link_libraries(ml_project ${FLASHLIGHT_LIBRARIES})
```

We then navigate to your build directory and compile the code:

```
cd ~/ml_project/build
cmake ..
make
```

Next, execute the compiled binary:

```
./ml_project
```

The possible output is:

```
Loss: 2.30258
```

Here, the loss value might vary due to the random initialization but should be around 2.3 for a 10-class problem with random inputs.

Dissecting Program Code

Let's now look in more detail at what our program actually does:

- We simulate input data and target labels because we're not yet loading the actual dataset. This allows us to focus on the mechanics of building and training a model.
- Our model is a simple neural network consisting of:
    - A **flattening layer** that reshapes the input tensor from a 3D image to a 1D vector.
    - A **linear layer** that maps the input features to the output classes.
- We pass the input data through the model to obtain the output predictions.
- The categorical cross-entropy loss function measures the discrepancy between the predicted outputs and the true targets.
- We perform backpropagation to compute gradients and then update the model's parameters using the optimizer.

- The program then prints the loss value, confirming that the computations are being performed correctly.

Now that we've successfully written and executed our first C++ machine learning program using Flashlight, we're ready to tackle more advanced topics. In the next chapter, we will focus on loading and preprocessing the actual CIFAR-10 dataset, moving from simulated data to real-world images.

Summary

In a nutshell, we're now on our way to learning about practical machine learning. We started off by showing how quickly machine learning is advancing and how much of an impact it can have on programmers. We learned about how C++ can help with machine learning, focusing on how it works well and the great libraries like Flashlight that are available.

We also introduced the CIFAR-10 dataset, which we will be using throughout this book to show how different machine learning techniques can be applied. Next, we set up the development environment on a Linux system, making sure we had all the tools and libraries we needed. Finally, we wrote our first C++ machine learning program using Flashlight. That way, we could make sure our setup worked and get a hands-on introduction to building and training a simple neural network. Once we've got this down, we can start looking into more advanced topics like data handling, modelling and machine learning.

CHAPTER 2: DATA HANDLING AND PREPROCESSING

Chapter Overview

Let's kick things off with chapter 2, where we will go over the key steps of prepping data for machine learning models. We will start by looking at how to load the CIFAR-10 dataset into our C++ program, getting to grips with its structure and how to access the images and labels. Next, we will look at data normalization and standardization techniques to make sure our model trains effectively by having input data that's properly scaled.

Then, we will learn about data augmentation techniques like flipping, cropping, and rotating images to artificially expand our dataset and improve model generalization. We will also look at how to create efficient data loaders in Flashlight, to handle data in batches and streamline the training process. Once we've got a handle on these topics, we will be ready to develop robust machine learning models that can handle real-world data complexities.

Loading CIFAR-10 Dataset

CIFAR-10 Dataset Overview

Before we dive into loading the CIFAR-10 dataset, we will briefly revisit what it is. The CIFAR-10 dataset is a collection of 60,000 color images, each sized at 32x32 pixels, categorized into 10 distinct classes. Each class represents a real-world object such as airplanes, cars, birds, cats, and so on. This dataset is widely used for training and benchmarking machine learning models in image classification tasks.

The dataset can be downloaded from https://www.cs.toronto.edu/~kriz/cifar-10-binary.tar.gz

The CIFAR-10 dataset is provided in a binary format, where each file contains a certain number of images and their corresponding labels. Each image is stored as a flat array of bytes, and understanding how to parse this format is essential for loading the data into our C++ program.

Downloading Dataset

So, since we have downloaded and extracted the dataset during the environment setup, the files should be located in the **~/ml_project/data/cifar-10-batches-bin** directory. If not, you can download and extract it using the following commands:

```
cd ~/ml_project/data
wget https://www.cs.toronto.edu/~kriz/cifar-10-binary.tar.gz
tar -xvzf cifar-10-binary.tar.gz
```

Here, each binary file in the dataset contains several images and labels. Specifically:

- The first byte in each sample is the label (0-9).

- The next 3072 bytes are the image pixels (32x32 pixels x 3 color channels).
- And, each image is stored in row-major order, and the color channels are stored sequentially.

Creating Data Loader Class

To efficiently load and manage the dataset, we will create a **CIFAR10Loader** class that reads the binary files and parses the data into usable formats.

Here, we first create a header file to define the class:

```
#ifndef CIFAR10_LOADER_H
#define CIFAR10_LOADER_H
#include <string>
#include <vector>
#include <tuple>
#include <flashlight/flashlight.h>
class CIFAR10Loader {
public:
    CIFAR10Loader(const std::string& data_dir, bool train =
true);
    std::vector<std::tuple<fl::Tensor, int>> getData();
private:
    std::string dataDir;
    bool isTrain;
    std::vector<std::string> files;
    std::vector<std::tuple<fl::Tensor, int>> data;
    void loadData();
};
#endif // CIFAR10_LOADER_H
```

Next, we implement the class methods as below.

```
#include "cifar10_loader.h"
#include <fstream>
```

```
#include <iostream>
CIFAR10Loader::CIFAR10Loader(const std::string& data_dir, bool
train)
    : dataDir(data_dir), isTrain(train) {
    if (isTrain) {
        for (int i = 1; i <= 5; ++i) {
            files.push_back(dataDir + "/data_batch_" +
std::to_string(i) + ".bin");
        }
    } else {
        files.push_back(dataDir + "/test_batch.bin");
    }
    loadData();
}
void CIFAR10Loader::loadData() {
    const int imageSize = 32 * 32 * 3; // 3072 bytes per image
    for (const auto& file : files) {
        std::ifstream inFile(file, std::ios::binary);
        if (!inFile.is_open()) {
            std::cerr << "Failed to open file: " << file <<
std::endl;
            continue;
        }
        while (inFile.peek() != EOF) {
            unsigned char label;
            inFile.read((char*)&label, 1);
            std::vector<unsigned char> buffer(imageSize);
            inFile.read((char*)buffer.data(), imageSize);
            // Convert buffer to Tensor
```

```
            fl::Tensor image = fl::Tensor::fromVector({3, 32,
32}, buffer);
            // Normalize pixel values to [0, 1]
            image = image.astype(fl::dtype::f32) / 255.0;
            // Store the image and label
            data.emplace_back(image, static_cast<int>(label));
        }
        inFile.close();
    }
}
std::vector<std::tuple<fl::Tensor, int>>
CIFAR10Loader::getData() {
    return data;
}
```

Integrate Data Loader into Program

Now, we will integrate this data loader into our main program. For this, we will update the project structure by including the header file. And to do that, we place the **cifar10_loader.h** and **cifar10_loader.cpp** files in the **include** and **src** directories, respectively.

```
~/ml_project/
            ├── CMakeLists.txt
            ├── data/
            ├── include/
            │       └── cifar10_loader.h
            ├── src/
                  ├── main.cpp
                  └── cifar10_loader.cpp
```

Next, update the **CMakeLists.txt** to include the new source file:

```
cmake_minimum_required(VERSION 3.10)
```

```
project(MLProject)
set(CMAKE_CXX_STANDARD 17)
find_package(flashlight REQUIRED)
include_directories(${FLASHLIGHT_INCLUDE_DIRS})
include_directories(${CMAKE_SOURCE_DIR}/include)
link_directories(${FLASHLIGHT_LIBRARY_DIRS})
add_executable(ml_project src/main.cpp src/cifar10_loader.cpp)
target_link_libraries(ml_project ${FLASHLIGHT_LIBRARIES})
```

Compiling and Running the Program

In order to compile, we first modify **main.cpp** to use the **CIFAR10Loader** class.

```
#include <flashlight/flashlight.h>
#include <iostream>
#include "cifar10_loader.h"
int main() {
    // Specify the path to the CIFAR-10 data directory
    std::string dataDir = "../data/cifar-10-batches-bin";
    // Create an instance of the CIFAR10Loader
    CIFAR10Loader loader(dataDir, true); // 'true' for
training data
    // Retrieve the data
    auto dataset = loader.getData();
    // Check the size of the dataset
    std::cout << "Total training samples: " << dataset.size()
<< std::endl;
    // Access the first sample
    auto [image, label] = dataset[0];
    // Print label
    std::cout << "Label of first image: " << label <<
std::endl;
```

```
    // Display image dimensions
    std::cout << "Image dimensions: " << image.shape() <<
std::endl;
    // Continue with the rest of your code...
    return 0;
}
```

We then build the project from the build directory:

```
cd ~/ml_project/build
cmake ..
make
```

Next, run the program as below:

```
./ml_project
```

Following is the possible output you can expect:

```
Total training samples: 50000
Label of first image: 6
Image dimensions: [3 32 32]
```

Now that we've got the CIFAR-10 dataset loaded into our C++ program, we can move on to preprocessing the data. Next, We will look at data normalization and standardization, which are key steps in getting the data ready for training machine learning models.

Data Normalization and Standardization

Why Data Normalization?

Data normalization is the process of scaling individual samples to have a unit norm. In the context of image data, normalization often involves adjusting the pixel values to a common scale, typically between 0 and 1, or transforming them to have a mean of zero and a standard deviation of one. This process helps in accelerating the training of neural networks and can lead to better convergence.

The benefit f normalizing the data are as below:

- Normalizing data reduces the risk of numerical instability in computations, especially when working with activation functions that are sensitive to input magnitude.
- Models often converge faster when the input features are on a similar scale, as it allows for more consistent weight updates during training.
- For activation functions like Sigmoid or Tanh, inputs with large magnitudes can lead to saturation, where the gradient becomes very small. Normalization mitigates this issue.

Implementing Data Normalization

To begin with, we will update our **CIFAR10Loader** to include data normalization. We will add the normalization steps after loading the image data.

```
// Normalize pixel values to [0, 1]
image = image.astype(fl::dtype::f32) / 255.0;
```

For your knowledge, we've already included this step in the previous code. However, to standardize the data further, we will compute the mean and standard deviation of the dataset and normalize accordingly.

Calculating Mean and Standard Deviation

To perform standardization, we need to calculate the mean and standard deviation across the dataset. For this, we modify the **loadData()** method to compute the mean and standard deviation.

```
void CIFAR10Loader::loadData() {
    const int imageSize = 32 * 32 * 3; // 3072 bytes per image
    fl::Tensor sum = fl::full({3, 32, 32}, 0.0);
    fl::Tensor sumSq = fl::full({3, 32, 32}, 0.0);
    int sampleCount = 0;
    for (const auto& file : files) {
        std::ifstream inFile(file, std::ios::binary);
        if (!inFile.is_open()) {
            std::cerr << "Failed to open file: " << file <<
std::endl;
            continue;
        }
        while (inFile.peek() != EOF) {
```

```
            unsigned char label;
            inFile.read((char*)&label, 1);
            std::vector<unsigned char> buffer(imageSize);
            inFile.read((char*)buffer.data(), imageSize);
            // Convert buffer to Tensor
            fl::Tensor image = fl::Tensor::fromVector({3, 32,
32}, buffer);
            // Convert to float and normalize to [0, 1]
            image = image.astype(fl::dtype::f32) / 255.0;
            // Accumulate sum and sum of squares
            sum += image;
            sumSq += image * image;
            ++sampleCount;
            // Store the image and label
            data.emplace_back(image, static_cast<int>(label));
        }
        inFile.close();
    }
    // Compute mean and std deviation
    fl::Tensor mean = sum / sampleCount;
    fl::Tensor variance = (sumSq / sampleCount) - (mean *
mean);
    fl::Tensor stddev = fl::sqrt(variance);
    // Normalize the dataset
    for (auto& sample : data) {
        fl::Tensor& img = std::get<0>(sample);
        img = (img - mean) / stddev;
    }
}
```

Here, to prevent division by zero in case of zero standard deviation, we do add a small epsilon value:

```
fl::Tensor epsilon = fl::full({3, 32, 32}, 1e-7);
fl::Tensor stddev = fl::sqrt(variance) + epsilon;
```

Verifying Normalization

After normalizing, the dataset should have a mean close to zero and a standard deviation close to one. We can simply add the following code to verify this:

```
void CIFAR10Loader::verifyNormalization() {
    fl::Tensor totalMean = fl::full({3, 32, 32}, 0.0);
    fl::Tensor totalStd = fl::full({3, 32, 32}, 0.0);
    for (const auto& sample : data) {
        const fl::Tensor& img = std::get<0>(sample);
        totalMean += img;
        totalStd += img * img;
    }
    totalMean = totalMean / data.size();
    fl::Tensor variance = (totalStd / data.size()) -
(totalMean * totalMean);
    fl::Tensor stddev = fl::sqrt(variance);
    std::cout << "Dataset Mean after normalization: " <<
totalMean.scalar<float>() << std::endl;
    std::cout << "Dataset Std Dev after normalization: " <<
stddev.scalar<float>() << std::endl;
}
verifyNormalization();
```

And then finally, rebuild and run the project:

```
cd ~/ml_project/build
cmake ..
make
```

```
./ml_project
```

You must get the following output:

```
Total training samples: 50000
Label of first image: 6
Image dimensions: [3 32 32]
Dataset Mean after normalization: -4.04449e-08
Dataset Std Dev after normalization: 0.999998
```

In the above output, the mean is close to zero, and the standard deviation is close to one. This indicates successful normalization.

Data Augmentation Techniques

Data augmentation is a technique that makes use of random data transformations to artificially increase both the size and diversity of your training dataset. Data augmentation copies what might happen in the real world to data, like changes in lighting, orientation, or scale. I've found this is really helpful in machine learning, especially when I'm working with image data and deep learning models. The more variability we add to the dataset, the better the model can generalize to new data, which helps avoid overfitting.

Common Data Augmentation Methods

Some common augmentation methods are rotation, flipping, cropping, scaling, and adding noise to the images.

Rotation

Rotating images by a certain angle helps the model recognize objects regardless of their orientation. For example, rotating an image of a car by 15 degrees should still allow the model to identify it as a car.

Flipping

Flipping images horizontally or vertically introduces mirror images into the dataset. This is useful when the orientation doesn't change the class of the object, such as in images of animals or vehicles.

Cropping

Random cropping involves selecting a random portion of the image and resizing it to the original dimensions. This simulates zooming in on the image and helps the model focus on different parts of the object.

Scaling

Adjusting the size of the image can help the model recognize objects at different scales. Scaling can be applied uniformly or non-uniformly to simulate distance variations.

Translation

Shifting the image along the X or Y axis helps the model recognize objects that are not centered in the frame.

Adding Noise

Introducing random noise can make the model more robust to grainy or low-quality images.

Now, we will try to integrate data augmentation techniques into our existing **CIFAR10Loader** class. This will allow us to apply transformations like rotation, flipping, and cropping to our images during the data loading process.

Implementing Data Augmentation

So here first, we will modify our **CIFAR10Loader** class to include augmentation functionality.

```
#ifndef CIFAR10_LOADER_H
#define CIFAR10_LOADER_H
#include <string>
#include <vector>
#include <tuple>
#include <flashlight/flashlight.h>
class CIFAR10Loader {
public:
    CIFAR10Loader(const std::string& data_dir, bool train =
true);
    std::vector<std::tuple<fl::Tensor, int>> getData();
    void enableAugmentation(bool enable);
private:
```

```
    std::string dataDir;
    bool isTrain;
    bool augment;
    std::vector<std::string> files;
    std::vector<std::tuple<fl::Tensor, int>> data;
    void loadData();
    fl::Tensor augmentImage(const fl::Tensor& image);
};
#endif // CIFAR10_LOADER_H
```

Next, we will implement the augmentation methods in **cifar10_loader.cpp**

```
#include "cifar10_loader.h"
#include <fstream>
#include <iostream>
#include <random>
CIFAR10Loader::CIFAR10Loader(const std::string& data_dir, bool
train)
    : dataDir(data_dir), isTrain(train), augment(false) {
    if (isTrain) {
        for (int i = 1; i <= 5; ++i) {
            files.push_back(dataDir + "/data_batch_" +
std::to_string(i) + ".bin");
        }
    } else {
        files.push_back(dataDir + "/test_batch.bin");
    }
    loadData();
}
void CIFAR10Loader::enableAugmentation(bool enable) {
    augment = enable;
```

```
}
void CIFAR10Loader::loadData() {
    const int imageSize = 32 * 32 * 3;
    for (const auto& file : files) {
        std::ifstream inFile(file, std::ios::binary);
        if (!inFile.is_open()) {
            std::cerr << "Failed to open file: " << file <<
std::endl;
            continue;
        }
        while (inFile.peek() != EOF) {
            unsigned char label;
            inFile.read((char*)&label, 1);
            std::vector<unsigned char> buffer(imageSize);
            inFile.read((char*)buffer.data(), imageSize);
            // Convert buffer to Tensor
            fl::Tensor image = fl::Tensor::fromVector({3, 32,
32}, buffer);
            image = image.astype(fl::dtype::f32) / 255.0;
            // Apply augmentation if enabled
            if (augment && isTrain) {
                image = augmentImage(image);
            }
            data.emplace_back(image, static_cast<int>(label));
        }
        inFile.close();
    }
}
fl::Tensor CIFAR10Loader::augmentImage(const fl::Tensor&
image) {
```

```
    fl::Tensor augmented = image.copy();
    // Random number generators
    static std::random_device rd;
    static std::mt19937 gen(rd());
    // Horizontal Flip
    std::bernoulli_distribution flip_dist(0.5); // 50% chance to flip
    if (flip_dist(gen)) {
        augmented = fl::flip(augmented, {2}); // Flip along the width axis
    }
    // Random Rotation
    std::uniform_real_distribution<> angle_dist(-15.0, 15.0); // Rotate between -15 and 15 degrees
    double angle = angle_dist(gen);
    augmented = fl::rotate(augmented, angle);
    // Random Cropping
    int cropSize = 28;
    std::uniform_int_distribution<> offset_dist(0, 32 - cropSize);
    int x_offset = offset_dist(gen);
    int y_offset = offset_dist(gen);
    augmented = augmented(
        fl::range(0, 3),
        fl::range(y_offset, y_offset + cropSize),
        fl::range(x_offset, x_offset + cropSize)
    );
    augmented = fl::resize(augmented, 32, 32);
    return augmented;
}
```

```
std::vector<std::tuple<fl::Tensor, int>>
CIFAR10Loader::getData() {
    return data;
}
```

Now here, the functions **fl::rotate** and **fl::resize** may not be available directly in Flashlight. If not, you may need to implement these functions or use alternative methods. For the purposes of this illustration, we will assume they exist.

Now next, in the **main.cpp**, we will enable augmentation and observe the changes.

```
#include <flashlight/flashlight.h>
#include <iostream>
#include "cifar10_loader.h"
int main() {
    // Specify the data directory
    std::string dataDir = "../data/cifar-10-batches-bin";
    // Initialize the data loader with augmentation enabled
    CIFAR10Loader loader(dataDir, true);
    loader.enableAugmentation(true);
    // Retrieve the data
    auto dataset = loader.getData();
    // Access a sample to verify augmentation
    auto [image, label] = dataset[0];
    // Display image dimensions after augmentation
    std::cout << "Image dimensions after augmentation: " <<
image.shape() << std::endl;
    // Proceed with model training...
    return 0;
}
```

And then finally, you compile and run the program as we did in the previous section. The entire idea is to apply these transformations randomly during training, which gives the model a slightly different dataset each epoch. This helps it to generalise better.

Creating Data Loaders

Efficient data loading is crucial for training machine learning models effectively. Flashlight provides dataset utilities that facilitate batch processing, shuffling, and multi-threaded data loading.

We will leverage Flashlight's **Dataset** classes to create a data loader that can handle batch processing efficiently.

Creating Custom Dataset Class

We need to create a custom dataset class that inherits from **fl::Dataset** and implements the required methods.

- Create **cifar10_dataset.h**

```
#ifndef CIFAR10_DATASET_H
#define CIFAR10_DATASET_H
#include <flashlight/dataset/dataset.h>
#include <flashlight/flashlight.h>
#include <vector>
#include <tuple>
class CIFAR10Dataset : public fl::Dataset {
public:
    CIFAR10Dataset(const std::vector<std::tuple<fl::Tensor,
int>>& data, bool augment = false);
    std::vector<fl::Tensor> get(const int64_t idx) const
override;
    int64_t size() const override;
private:
    std::vector<std::tuple<fl::Tensor, int>> data_;
    bool augment_;
    fl::Tensor augmentImage(const fl::Tensor& image) const;
};
#endif // CIFAR10_DATASET_H
```

- Implement **cifar10_dataset.cpp**

```
#include "cifar10_dataset.h"
#include <random>
CIFAR10Dataset::CIFAR10Dataset(const
std::vector<std::tuple<fl::Tensor, int>>& data, bool augment)
    : data_(data), augment_(augment) {}
std::vector<fl::Tensor> CIFAR10Dataset::get(const int64_t idx)
const {
    auto [image, label] = data_[idx];
    if (augment_) {
        image = augmentImage(image);
    }
    fl::Tensor labelTensor =
fl::fromScalar(static_cast<float>(label));
    return {image, labelTensor};
}
int64_t CIFAR10Dataset::size() const {
    return data_.size();
}
fl::Tensor CIFAR10Dataset::augmentImage(const fl::Tensor&
image) const {
    // Implement augmentation similar to the loader
    fl::Tensor augmented = image.copy();
    static thread_local std::mt19937
gen(std::random_device{}());
    // Horizontal Flip
    std::bernoulli_distribution flip_dist(0.5);
    if (flip_dist(gen)) {
        augmented = fl::flip(augmented, {2});
    }
```

```
    // Additional augmentations can be added here
    return augmented;
}
```

Creating DataLoader

Next, We will use Flashlight's data loader utilities to create a data loader that handles batching and shuffling. We can simply do this by updating **main.cpp**

```
#include <flashlight/flashlight.h>
#include <iostream>
#include "cifar10_loader.h"
#include "cifar10_dataset.h"
int main() {
    // Load data using CIFAR10Loader
    std::string dataDir = "../data/cifar-10-batches-bin";
    CIFAR10Loader loader(dataDir, true);
    auto dataset = loader.getData();
    // Create a custom dataset
    CIFAR10Dataset cifarDataset(dataset, true); // Enable
augmentation
    // Create a batch dataset
    int batchSize = 64;
    auto batchDataset = fl::BatchDataset(
        std::make_shared<CIFAR10Dataset>(cifarDataset),
        batchSize
    );
    // Shuffle the dataset
    auto shuffledDataset = fl::ShuffleDataset(batchDataset);
    // Use a threaded data loader
    auto dataLoader = fl::PrefetchDataset(shuffledDataset, /*
numThreads */ 4);
```

```
    // Iterate over the data loader
    for (auto& batch : *dataLoader) {
        auto inputs = batch[0];  // Batch of images
        auto targets = batch[1]; // Batch of labels
        // Proceed with training...
        std::cout << "Batch inputs shape: " << inputs.shape()
<< std::endl;
        std::cout << "Batch targets shape: " <<
targets.shape() << std::endl;
        break; // For demonstration, process only one batch
    }
    return 0;
}
```

After this, finally, you compile and run the program. To sum up, classes like **BatchDataset**, **ShuffleDataset**, and **PrefetchDataset** helped us optimize our data pipeline for batch processing and parallel loading.

Summary

To wrap up, we zeroed in on the most important parts of data handling and preprocessing in machine learning. We started by loading the CIFAR-10 dataset into our project, parsing binary data files using C++ streams, and organizing the data into efficient structures. This hands-on approach gave us the skills we need to manage real-world datasets effectively.

Next, we implemented data normalization and standardization techniques to make sure our input data is scaled correctly for optimal model performance. I'd like to emphasize that these preprocessing steps are essential for enhancing the convergence and accuracy of neural networks. We also looked at data augmentation techniques like rotation, flipping, and cropping. By using these techniques, we made our dataset bigger, which helped our model learn more and reduced the risk of overfitting. We added these changes to our data pipeline, so they're now part of the training process.

Finally, we learned how to create fast data loaders using Flashlight's dataset tools. Now we can handle batch processing and multithreaded data loading, which makes our training workflow more efficient and ensures that data is fed into our models quickly.

CHAPTER 3: BUILDING A SIMPLE NEURAL NETWORK

Chapter Overview

This chapter is just going to walk you practically through the process of building neural networks. We will start by going over the basics of neural networks again to make sure we're all on the same page about how they work and process information. This includes concepts like neurons, activation functions, and the structure of layers that allow networks to learn from data patterns.

Next, we will put together a simple feedforward neural network, turning theoretical concepts into practical code. We will use the Flashlight library to put together the model architecture by adding layers to make a network that works. This hands-on exercise will help you understand how to build models and how to put neural networks into practice with C++.

Finally, we will look at forward propagation, where we will pass input data through the network to generate predictions. This is really important for training and evaluating our model's performance. By the end of this chapter, You will have built a basic neural network that can make predictions on the CIFAR-10 dataset, which is a great start for more advanced models in future chapters.

Neural Network Key Components

Neural networks are computational models inspired by the human brain's interconnected network of neurons. They consist of layers of nodes (neurons) that process input data to recognize patterns and make decisions. Neural networks are foundational to deep learning and are widely used in various applications such as image recognition, natural language processing, and time series prediction.

Neurons, Layers, Weights and Biases

Neurons are the basic processing units of a neural network. Each neuron receives input, applies a transformation, and passes the output to the next layer. Neural networks are organized into layers:

- **Input Layer:** Receives the initial data.
- **Hidden Layers:** Perform computations and extract features.
- **Output Layer:** Produces the final result or prediction.

Weights determine the strength of the connection between neurons. Biases allow the activation function to shift, enabling the network to model complex relationships.

Activation and Loss Functions

Activation functions introduce non-linearity into the network, allowing it to learn complex patterns. Common activation functions include:

- **Sigmoid:** Maps input values to a range between 0 and 1.
- **ReLU (Rectified Linear Unit):** Outputs zero for negative inputs and the input itself for positive inputs.
- **Tanh:** Maps input values to a range between -1 and 1.

The loss function measures the difference between the network's predictions and the actual targets. Minimizing the loss function during training improves the model's accuracy.

Optimization Algorithms

Optimizers adjust the network's weights and biases to minimize the loss function. Common optimizers include:

- Stochastic Gradient Descent (SGD)
- Adam

There are different types of neural networks, apart from the core components. These include recurrent neural networks, convolutional neural networks and, most important of all, feedforward neural networks. As a foundation, feedforward networks are the most important. Then we have CNNs and RNNs, which extend capabilities to images and sequential data, respectively.

Implementing a Feedforward Network

Feedforward neural networks, also known as multilayer perceptrons (MLPs), are the simplest type of neural networks where connections between the nodes do not form cycles. Information moves in only one direction—from the input layer, through hidden layers, to the output layer.

Now here, we will build a MLP from scratch. To begin with, we will create a new class for our MLP and integrate it into our existing project as per the following steps.

- Creating the MLP Class with the header file **`simple_mlp.h`**

```
#ifndef SIMPLE_MLP_H
#define SIMPLE_MLP_H
#include <flashlight/flashlight.h>
class SimpleMLP {
public:
    SimpleMLP(int inputSize, int hiddenSize, int outputSize);
    fl::Variable forward(const fl::Variable& input);
```

```
    std::vector<fl::Variable> getParameters();
private:
    std::shared_ptr<fl::Linear> fc1_;
    std::shared_ptr<fl::Linear> fc2_;
    std::shared_ptr<fl::Linear> fc3_;
};
#endif // SIMPLE_MLP_H
```

Next, we implement in **simple_mlp.cpp**

```
#include "simple_mlp.h"
SimpleMLP::SimpleMLP(int inputSize, int hiddenSize, int
outputSize) {
    // Initialize layers
    fc1_ = std::make_shared<fl::Linear>(inputSize,
hiddenSize);
    fc2_ = std::make_shared<fl::Linear>(hiddenSize,
hiddenSize);
    fc3_ = std::make_shared<fl::Linear>(hiddenSize,
outputSize);
}
fl::Variable SimpleMLP::forward(const fl::Variable& input) {
    // Forward pass through the network
    auto out = fc1_->forward(input);
    out = fl::relu(out);
    out = fc2_->forward(out);
    out = fl::relu(out);
    out = fc3_->forward(out);
    return out;
}
std::vector<fl::Variable> SimpleMLP::getParameters() {
    // Collect parameters from all layers
```

```
    std::vector<fl::Variable> params;
    params.insert(params.end(), fc1_->params().begin(), fc1_-
>params().end());
    params.insert(params.end(), fc2_->params().begin(), fc2_-
>params().end());
    params.insert(params.end(), fc3_->params().begin(), fc3_-
>params().end());
    return params;
}
```

- Update the **main.cpp** to include the new MLP class.

```
#include <flashlight/flashlight.h>
#include <iostream>
#include "cifar10_loader.h"
#include "cifar10_dataset.h"
#include "simple_mlp.h"
int main() {
    // Load training data
    std::string dataDir = "../data/cifar-10-batches-bin";
    CIFAR10Loader loader(dataDir, true);
    auto dataset = loader.getData();
    // Create dataset and data loader
    CIFAR10Dataset cifarDataset(dataset, true);
    int batchSize = 64;
    auto batchDataset = fl::BatchDataset(
        std::make_shared<CIFAR10Dataset>(cifarDataset),
        batchSize
    );
    auto dataLoader = fl::PrefetchDataset(batchDataset, /*
numThreads */ 4);
```

```
    // Define network architecture
    int inputSize = 32 * 32 * 3; // Flattened image size
    int hiddenSize = 128;
    int outputSize = 10; // Number of classes
    SimpleMLP model(inputSize, hiddenSize, outputSize);
    // Define loss function and optimizer
    auto criterion = fl::CategoricalCrossEntropy();
    fl::SGDOptimizer optimizer(model.getParameters(), 0.01);
// Learning rate of 0.01
    // Training loop
    int numEpochs = 5;
    for (int epoch = 1; epoch <= numEpochs; ++epoch) {
        std::cout << "Epoch " << epoch << "/" << numEpochs <<
std::endl;
        int batchIndex = 0;
        for (auto& batch : *dataLoader) {
            auto inputs = batch[0];  // Batch of images
            auto targets = batch[1]; // Batch of labels
            // Flatten inputs
            inputs = fl::reshape(inputs, {inputSize,
batchSize});
            // Convert to Variables
            fl::Variable inputVar(inputs, false);
            fl::Variable targetVar(targets, false);
            // Forward pass
            auto outputs = model.forward(inputVar);
            // Compute loss
            auto loss = criterion(outputs, targetVar);
            // Backward pass and update
            optimizer.zeroGrad();
```

```
            loss.backward();
            optimizer.step();
            // Print loss every 100 batches
            if (batchIndex % 100 == 0) {
                std::cout << "Batch " << batchIndex << ",
Loss: " << loss.scalar<float>() << std::endl;
            }
            batchIndex++;
        }
    }
    return 0;
}
```

- Add the new source files to your **CMakeLists.txt**.

```
add_executable(ml_project
    src/main.cpp
    src/cifar10_loader.cpp
    src/cifar10_dataset.cpp
    src/simple_mlp.cpp
)
```

And then finally, you compile and run the program.

```
cd ~/ml_project/build
cmake ..
make
./ml_project
```

You may expect the following output:

```
Epoch 1/5
Batch 0, Loss: 2.30258
```

```
Batch 100, Loss: 2.30147
...
```

In the upcoming sections, we will explore implementing CNNs to improve our model's performance on image data like CIFAR-10. We will also delve into more advanced concepts like backpropagation implementation and optimization techniques.

Defining Model Architecture

So here, we will delve deeper into Flashlight's API to define the layers and structure of our neural network more efficiently and flexibly. To let you know that Flashlight offers container classes like **Sequential**, **Container**, and **Module**, which allow us to stack layers and create modular architectures as below:

- **`fl::Sequential`:** A container that feeds the output of one module directly into the next. It's ideal for creating feedforward networks where layers are applied in sequence.
- **`fl::Container`:** An abstract class that can hold multiple modules and provides flexibility in defining custom forward passes.
- **`fl::Module`:** The base class for all neural network layers in Flashlight.

Now, instead of manually managing each layer, we can use **fl::Sequential** to build our MLP more concisely. For this, we will redefine our **SimpleMLP** class to inherit from **fl::Sequential** in the header file **simple_mlp.h**

```
#ifndef SIMPLE_MLP_H
#define SIMPLE_MLP_H
#include <flashlight/flashlight.h>
class SimpleMLP : public fl::Sequential {
public:
    SimpleMLP(int inputSize, int hiddenSize, int outputSize);
};
#endif // SIMPLE_MLP_H
```

Next, add the following in the implementation file **simple_mlp.cpp**

```
#include "simple_mlp.h"
```

```
SimpleMLP::SimpleMLP(int inputSize, int hiddenSize, int
outputSize) {
    // Add layers to the Sequential container
    add(fl::View({inputSize})); // Flatten the input
    add(fl::Linear(inputSize, hiddenSize));
    add(fl::ReLU());
    add(fl::Linear(hiddenSize, hiddenSize));
    add(fl::ReLU());
    add(fl::Linear(hiddenSize, outputSize));
    add(fl::LogSoftmax());
}
```

In the above script,

- **`add(fl::View({inputSize}));`** reshapes the input tensor to the specified shape. Here, we flatten the input image into a 1D vector.
- **`add(fl::Linear(inputSize, hiddenSize));`** adds a fully connected linear layer that transforms the input size to the hidden layer size.
- **`add(fl::ReLU());`** applies the ReLU activation function to introduce non-linearity.
- **`add(fl::Linear(hiddenSize, outputSize));`** maps the hidden representations to the output classes.
- **`add(fl::LogSoftmax());`** applies the LogSoftmax function to the output, which is suitable when using the negative log-likelihood loss.

Th final steps is to update the training code in **main.cpp**.

```
// Define network architecture
int inputSize = 32 * 32 * 3; // Flattened image size
int hiddenSize = 128;
int outputSize = 10; // Number of classes
SimpleMLP model(inputSize, hiddenSize, outputSize);
// Get model parameters
auto params = model.params();
```

```
// Define loss function and optimizer
auto criterion = fl::NegativeLogLikelihood();
fl::SGDOptimizer optimizer(params, 0.01);
```

Since we used **LogSoftmax** in the final layer, we switch to the negative log-likelihood loss (**fl::NegativeLogLikelihood()**), which is compatible with **LogSoftmax**. The **model.params()** retrieves all the learnable parameters from the model.

Forward Propagation Implementation

We now move to the next learning i.e. implementing the forward propagation logic. Now here, forward propagation is the process of passing input data through the network layers to obtain an output.

In forward propagation:

- The input data is prepared and, if necessary, reshaped to match the network's expected input dimensions.
- The input is passed through each layer sequentially.
- Each layer performs a computation, such as a linear transformation or activation function.
- The final output layer produces the network's predictions.

And now, we will implement the forward pass in our **main.cpp** using the updated model.

Preparing Input Data

In the training loop, we need to ensure that the input data is in the correct shape and format.

```
// Flatten inputs
inputs = fl::reshape(inputs, {inputSize, batchSize});
```

Here, the **inputs** originally has the shape **{3, 32, 32, batchSize}**. We reshape it to **{inputSize, batchSize}** where **inputSize = 3 * 32 * 32**.

Converting to Variables and Forward Pass

Flashlight uses the **fl::Variable** class to track operations for automatic differentiation.

```
// Convert to Variables
```

```
fl::Variable inputVar(inputs, false); // 'false' indicates no need for gradients on inputs
fl::Variable targetVar(targets, false); // Targets do not require gradients
// Forward pass
auto outputs = model.forward(inputVar);
```

Here,

- The **model.forward(inputVar)** passes the input variable through the network.
- The output is a **fl::Variable** containing the network's predictions.

Backward Pass and Parameter Updates

Although this is part of training rather than forward propagation, it's essential to see the complete picture.

```
// Backward pass and update
optimizer.zeroGrad();
loss.backward();
optimizer.step();
```

Here,

- **optimizer.zeroGrad()** clears previous gradients.
- **loss.backward();** computes gradients with respect to the loss.
- **optimizer.step();** updates model parameters based on gradients.

Monitoring Training Progress

To monitor the training process, try including print statements to monitor the loss and ensure the model is learning as below:

```
if (batchIndex % 100 == 0) {
    std::cout << "Epoch [" << epoch << "/" << numEpochs << "], Batch [" << batchIndex
              << "], Loss: " << loss.scalar<float>() << std::endl;
```

```
}
```

Evaluation using Forward Pass

To see how well the model works with new data, we run it through without changing the parameters.

```
// Evaluation mode
model.eval(); // Set the model to evaluation mode (if necessary)
// Forward pass on validation data
auto outputs = model.forward(inputVar);
// Compute predictions
auto predictions = fl::argmax(outputs, 0);
// Compare predictions with targets to compute accuracy
```

Here, for evaluation, we might disable certain layers like dropout by setting the model to evaluation mode.

Training Neural Network on CIFAR-10

Now that we've got our neural network architecture defined and the forward propagation implemented, it's time to train the model on the CIFAR-10 dataset. When we train, we set up a loop that goes over the data, calculates the loss, does backpropagation, and updates the model's parameters. We will also talk about how to keep an eye on the training process and make sense of the initial results.

Setting up Training Loop

A training loop typically involves multiple epochs, where an epoch is a full pass over the entire training dataset. Within each epoch, we iterate over mini-batches of data.

Following is how you can set up the training loop:

Defining Hyperparameters

First, we need to set some hyperparameters that control the training process.

```
int numEpochs = 10;
int batchSize = 64;
```

```
float learningRate = 0.01;
```

Here,

- **numEpochs** is the number of times the model will see the entire dataset.
- **batchSize** are the number of samples processed before the model's parameters are updated.
- **learningRate** controls how much the model is adjusted during each update.

Preparing Data Loader

We already have our **CIFAR10Dataset** and data loader set up. But we must ensure the batch size matches the one defined above.

```
// Create dataset and data loader
CIFAR10Dataset cifarDataset(dataset, true);
auto batchDataset = fl::BatchDataset(
    std::make_shared<CIFAR10Dataset>(cifarDataset),
    batchSize
);
auto dataLoader = fl::PrefetchDataset(batchDataset, /*
numThreads */ 4);
```

Initializing Model, Loss Function, and Optimizer

```
// Define network architecture
SimpleMLP model(inputSize, hiddenSize, outputSize);
// Get model parameters
auto params = model.params();
// Define loss function and optimizer
auto criterion = fl::NegativeLogLikelihood();
fl::SGDOptimizer optimizer(params, learningRate);
```

Implementing Training Loop

```
for (int epoch = 1; epoch <= numEpochs; ++epoch) {
```

```
    std::cout << "Epoch " << epoch << "/" << numEpochs <<
std::endl;
    int batchIndex = 0;
    float epochLoss = 0.0;
    int correct = 0;
    int total = 0;
    for (auto& batch : *dataLoader) {
        auto inputs = batch[0];  // Batch of images
        auto targets = batch[1]; // Batch of labels
        // Flatten inputs
        inputs = fl::reshape(inputs, {inputSize, batchSize});
        // Convert to Variables
        fl::Variable inputVar(inputs, false);
        fl::Variable targetVar(targets, false);
        // Forward pass
        auto outputs = model.forward(inputVar);
        // Compute loss
        auto loss = criterion(outputs, targetVar);
        // Backward pass and update
        optimizer.zeroGrad();
        loss.backward();
        optimizer.step();
        // Accumulate loss
        epochLoss += loss.scalar<float>();
        // Calculate accuracy
        auto predictions = fl::argmax(outputs.tensor(), 0);
        auto targetTensor =
targetVar.tensor().astype(fl::dtype::s32);
        correct += fl::count(predictions ==
targetTensor).asScalar<int>();
```

```
        total += batchSize;
        // Print loss every 100 batches
        if (batchIndex % 100 == 0) {
            std::cout << "Batch " << batchIndex << ", Loss: "
<< loss.scalar<float>() << std::endl;
        }
        batchIndex++;
    }
    // Compute average loss and accuracy for the epoch
    float avgLoss = epochLoss / batchIndex;
    float accuracy = static_cast<float>(correct) / total *
100.0f;
    std::cout << "Epoch " << epoch << " completed. Average
Loss: " << avgLoss
              << ", Accuracy: " << accuracy << "%" <<
std::endl;
}
```

Observing Initial Results

The way you train a neural network is by repeating the process a few times. At first, the model might not be as good as we'd like, but it should get better over time.

Let us consider the following sample output:

```
Epoch 1/10
Batch 0, Loss: 2.30258
Batch 100, Loss: 2.30147
Batch 200, Loss: 2.29895
...
Epoch 1 completed. Average Loss: 2.300, Accuracy: 12.5%
```

If we have to interpret the results, here:

- A gradual decrease in loss indicates that the model is learning.

- An increase in accuracy shows that the model is making better predictions.
- With a simple MLP on a complex dataset like CIFAR-10, progress may be slow.

Now here, to better understand the training process, consider plotting the loss and accuracy over epochs by adding the following code to record metrics:

```
std::vector<float> lossHistory;
std::vector<float> accuracyHistory;
// After each epoch
lossHistory.push_back(avgLoss);
accuracyHistory.push_back(accuracy);
```

After training, you can save these metrics to a file and use a tool like Python's Matplotlib to plot them. Here, we've learned how to monitor the training process by tracking loss and accuracy. While the MLP may not achieve high performance on CIFAR-10 due to its simplicity, this exercise provides strong insights into the training mechanics and prepares us for building deeper networks in subsequent chapters.

Summary

We started off by going over the basics of neural networks. We learned about neurons, layers, activation functions, and how they work together to create complex models that can learn from data. Next, we put together a feedforward neural network (MLP) from the ground up using C++ classes and the Flashlight library to define the architecture. This hands-on approach really helped us understand how the theory we'd learned could be put into practice in code.

Next, we used Flashlight's API to define the model architecture more efficiently, using containers like fl::Sequential to streamline the construction of our network. Once we'd implemented forward propagation, we could process the data and generate predictions. We also set up a training loop to train the MLP on the CIFAR-10 dataset. We saw the initial results and learned how to monitor the training process. All of this gave us a solid base for building and training neural networks. It also prepared us for more advanced topics in deep learning.

Chapter 4: Training Deep Neural Networks

Chapter Overview

In this chapter, we're going to look closely at training of deep neural networks. We will start by taking a look at the building blocks of a solid training loop. We will see how epochs, batches, and iterations fit into the model training process. It's important to understand these elements if we want to make sure our models learn effectively and optimize the training process. Next, we will learn about different loss functions and optimization algorithms. We will look at how different loss functions can be used in different situations and how optimization algorithms like SGD and Adam adjust the model's parameters to minimize the loss. Then, we will put backpropagation into practice, getting a better grasp on how gradients are calculated and how they affect the learning process.

Finally, we will use Flashlight's built-in optimizers to make the training process easier. We will learn how to use these optimizers with our models, adjust hyperparameters, and monitor their effects on training. By the end of this chapter, You will understand how to train deep neural networks and be ready to train more complex models efficiently.

Deep Dive Training Loops

It's not as simple as just feeding data into a neural network. To get the best results, you need to have a carefully structured loop that orchestrates the entire learning process. A solid training loop is key to ensuring the model learns from the data properly and gets to the best solution possible. We will take a look at the main parts of a training loop: **epochs**, **batches**, and **iterations**. We will see how they work together in the context of neural network training.

Epochs

An **epoch** is one complete pass through the entire training dataset. When training a neural network, it's rarely sufficient to expose the model to the data only once. Multiple epochs allow the model to learn and refine its parameters incrementally.

Why Multiple Epochs Are Necessary?

Each epoch is an important step in making the model learn better. It lets the model adjust its weights based on the data, which helps it to understand the underlying patterns better. Repeated exposure to the data means that the model's parameters gradually move towards values that minimise the loss function. Additionally, running multiple epochs helps the model to understand new, unseen data by reinforcing the learning process.

Determining Number of Epochs

It's super important to choose the right number of epochs when training a model. If you train the model too few times, it won't learn enough from the data to identify significant patterns. But if you train it too many times, it'll start to focus too much on the training data, including things like noise and outliers, which will make it less effective when it's used with new data. A good way to decide when to stop training is to monitor how well the model is doing on a validation set.

In our C++ project using Flashlight, we can define the number of epochs as follows:

```
int numEpochs = 10; // Training the model for 10 epochs
```

Batches

A **batch**, or **mini-batch**, is a subset of the training dataset used during one iteration of training. Instead of processing the entire dataset at once, which can be computationally intensive and may not fit into memory, we divide the data into smaller batches.

Advantages of Batches

The advantages of batches include several key benefits that enhance machine learning workflows. Smaller batches consume less memory, making it possible to train larger models or manage bigger datasets efficiently. They also facilitate faster computations by optimizing the use of hardware acceleration, significantly reducing training times. Additionally, the introduction of randomness through batching fosters better generalization by reducing the risk of the model overfitting to the training data.

Choosing Batch Size

I've found that choosing the right batch size is really important for effective model training. If you use a small batch size, you might get noisy gradient estimates, which can help you escape local minima, but You will probably need more iterations to achieve convergence. On the other hand, if you use a large batch size, You will get more accurate gradient estimates, but You will need more memory and it might take longer to train per epoch. It's about finding the right balance between these things to get the best results.

Following is a quick sample implementation of batches:

```
int batchSize = 64; // Using a batch size of 64 samples
```

Iterations

An **iteration** refers to one update of the model's parameters. During each iteration, the model processes one batch of data, computes the loss, performs backpropagation, and updates the parameters using an optimizer. The number of iterations per epoch is basically how many batches of data are processed in one go through the dataset. The calculation is pretty straightforward:

The formula for iterations per epoch is:

Iterations per Epoch = Total Number of Samples / Batch Size

Let's say there are 50,000 samples in total, and the batch size is set to 64. If we use the formula, we get this result:

Iterations per Epoch = 50,000 / 64 ≈ 782 iterations. That means we're looking at about 782 iterations to complete one epoch under these conditions.

Building Training Loop

We will now put it all together and build a training loop that incorporates epochs, batches, and iterations in following step-by-stepmanner:

- Initialize Model, Loss Function, and Optimizer

```
// Define network architecture
SimpleMLP model(inputSize, hiddenSize, outputSize);
// Get model parameters
auto params = model.params();
// Define loss function
auto criterion = fl::NegativeLogLikelihood();
// Define optimizer (e.g., SGD with learning rate 0.01)
float learningRate = 0.01;
fl::SGDOptimizer optimizer(params, learningRate);
```

- Training Over Epochs

Here, we loop over the number of epochs, allowing the model to learn from the data multiple times.

```
for (int epoch = 1; epoch <= numEpochs; ++epoch) {
    std::cout << "Starting epoch " << epoch << " of " <<
numEpochs << std::endl;
    // Initialize metrics for this epoch
    float epochLoss = 0.0;
    int correct = 0;
    int total = 0;
    // Training code for each epoch goes here
```

```
}
```

- Iterating Over Batches

Next within each epoch, we iterate over the batches provided by our data loader.

```
for (auto& batch : *dataLoader) {
    // Extract inputs and targets from the batch
    auto inputs = batch[0];  // Images
    auto targets = batch[1]; // Labels
    // Training code for each batch goes here
}
```

- Data Preparation

Then, we need to prepare the data before feeding it into the model.

```
// Flatten inputs to match the input size of the MLP
inputs = fl::reshape(inputs, {inputSize, batchSize});
// Convert inputs and targets to Variables
fl::Variable inputVar(inputs, false);    // 'false' indicates
no need for gradients on inputs
fl::Variable targetVar(targets, false);  // Targets do not
require gradients
```

- Forward Pass

We then pass the input data through the model to get predictions.

```
// Forward pass
auto outputs = model.forward(inputVar);
```

- Compute Loss

Next, we calculate the loss using the specified loss function.

```
// Compute loss
auto loss = criterion(outputs, targetVar);
```

- Backward Pass and Parameter Update

We then start to perform backpropagation to compute gradients and then update the model's parameters.

```
// Zero out gradients from the previous iteration
optimizer.zeroGrad();
// Backward pass to compute gradients
loss.backward();
// Update model parameters
optimizer.step();
```

- Monitoring Training Progress

Finally, we can accumulate metrics like loss and accuracy to monitor the model's performance.

```
// Accumulate loss
epochLoss += loss.scalar<float>();
// Compute accuracy
auto predictions = fl::argmax(outputs.tensor(), 0);
auto targetTensor = targetVar.tensor().astype(fl::dtype::s32);
correct += fl::count(predictions ==
targetTensor).asScalar<int>();
total += batchSize;
// Optionally, print progress every few iterations
if (iteration % 100 == 0) {
    std::cout << "Iteration " << iteration << ", Loss: " <<
loss.scalar<float>() << std::endl;
}
iteration++;
```

Now here, at the end of each epoch, we calculate and display the average loss and accuracy.

```
float avgLoss = epochLoss / iteration;
float accuracy = static_cast<float>(correct) / total * 100.0f;
```

```
std::cout << "Epoch " << epoch << " completed. Average Loss: "
<< avgLoss
            << ", Accuracy: " << accuracy << "%" << std::endl;
```

To improve the training process, we can incorporate several strategies, sich as:

- Data Shuffling
- Learning Rate Scheduling
- Early Stopping
- Checkpointing
- Validation Phase

By setting up the loop to include epochs, batches, and iterations, and by using techniques like learning rate scheduling and early stopping, we can make the training process as effective as possible. If we keep track of how the training and validation metrics are doing, we can make better decisions and tweaks to get models that perform well and generalize effectively.

Loss Functions and Optimization Algorithms

The training of neural networks hinges on two critical components: **loss functions** and **optimization algorithms**. The loss function measures how well the model's predictions match the actual targets, providing a signal for learning. The optimization algorithm uses this signal to adjust the model's parameters in a way that minimizes the loss. We will delve into common loss functions like cross-entropy and mean squared error, and explore optimization algorithms such as Stochastic Gradient Descent (SGD) and Adam. We will also discuss how these components have contributed to the development of neural networks.

Loss Functions

A **loss function** quantifies the discrepancy between the predicted outputs of the neural network and the actual target values. It provides a scalar value that the optimization algorithm aims to minimize during training.

Cross-Entropy Loss

Cross-entropy loss is widely used for classification tasks, especially when dealing with multiple classes. It measures the difference between two probability distributions: the true distribution (the actual labels) and the predicted distribution (the model's outputs).

Following is the formula for categorical cross-entropy loss:

$$\text{Loss} = -\sum_{i=1}^{N}\sum_{k=1}^{K} y_{i,k} \log(\hat{y}_{i,k})$$

Where:

- N is the number of samples.
- K is the number of classes.
- yi,k is 1 if sample i belongs to class k, and 0 otherwise.
- $y^\wedge i,k$ is the predicted probability that sample i belongs to class k.

Cross-entropy is a widely used loss function due to its sensitivity to prediction confidence. It penalizes incorrect predictions more heavily when the model exhibits high confidence in those predictions. This characteristic encourages the model to produce accurate probability estimates, improving overall reliability.

It is also highly compatible with the softmax activation function. The softmax function generates a probability distribution over different classes, making it an ideal match for cross-entropy. Together, they ensure effective training of models for classification tasks, leading to robust and well-calibrated predictions.

In our project, we can define the cross-entropy loss using Flashlight:

```
auto criterion = fl::CategoricalCrossEntropy();
```

Mean Squared Error (MSE)

Mean Squared Error is commonly used for regression tasks, where the goal is to predict continuous values. The following is the formula:

$$\text{MSE} = \frac{1}{N}\sum_{i=1}^{N}(y_i - \hat{y}_i)^2$$

Where:

- yi is the actual value.
- $y^\wedge i$ is the predicted value.

MSE places significant emphasis on larger errors by squaring the discrepancies. This approach ensures that larger deviations are penalized more severely, highlighting their impact on the overall error measurement. The smooth gradient offered by MSE is another crucial advantage. It provides a continuous and differentiable loss surface, which is essential for facilitating gradient-based optimization methods. This characteristic enables efficient model training and enhances the convergence of optimization algorithms.

Mean Absolute Error (MAE)

The MAE shows the average distance between what we predicted and what actually happened. This metric is a popular choice in regression analysis and model evaluation because it's easy to understand and effective.

MAE is calculated as follows:

$$\text{MAE} = \frac{1}{N}\sum_{i=1}^{N}|y_i - \hat{y}_i|$$

The MAE is calculated by taking the absolute value of the difference between the actual and predicted values for each observation. In the formula, N represents the total number of observations, yi is the actual value, and $y^\wedge i$ is the predicted value.

MAE is a good choice in many situations. It's less affected by outliers than MSE, so it's more stable. Plus, the error is in the same units as the target variable, which makes it easier to understand and gives a clearer picture of how the model is doing.

Optimization Algorithms

An **optimization algorithm** adjusts the model's parameters to minimize the loss function based on the computed gradients.

Stochastic Gradient Descent (SGD)

Stochastic Gradient Descent (SGD) updates the model's parameters by adjusting them in the direction opposite to the gradient of the loss function with respect to those parameters. The update rule can be expressed as:

$$\theta new = \theta old - \eta \nabla\theta L(\theta old)$$

In this equation, θ represents the model's parameters, η is the learning rate, and $\nabla\theta L(\theta)$ denotes the gradient of the loss function with respect to θ. The characteristics of SGD include its efficiency and stochasticity. It processes one batch at a time, making it particularly suitable for large datasets. The randomness introduced by its stochastic nature can help the model navigate towards a global minimum, bypassing potential traps in local minima.

However, SGD also presents certain challenges. Selecting an appropriate learning rate is critical. A learning rate that is too high may lead to divergence, while one that is too low can result in slow convergence. Additionally, SGD may encounter issues with convergence, particularly when dealing with local minima or saddle points.

SGD with Momentum

Momentum accelerates stochastic gradient descent (SGD) by incorporating a fraction of the previous update into the current update. This approach builds upon past gradients to smooth and accelerate the optimization process.

The update rule for momentum is as follows:

$$v = \gamma v_{\text{prev}} + \eta \nabla_\theta L(\theta)$$

$$\theta_{\text{new}} = \theta_{\text{old}} - v$$

Here,

v represents the velocity, which is the accumulated gradient. The term γ is the momentum coefficient, typically set between 0.9 and 0.99. This coefficient determines the influence of past updates on the current update.

The parameter $\eta\nabla\ \theta L(\theta)$ refers to the learning rate multiplied by the gradient of the loss function with respect to the parameters θ. The benefits of using momentum are significant. It enables faster convergence by promoting movement in relevant directions and mitigating oscillations in the optimization path. Additionally, momentum helps the optimizer overcome shallow local minima, allowing it to escape regions that might trap other optimization techniques.

Following is a quick example:

```
fl::SGDOptimizer optimizer(params, learningRate, 0.9); // 0.9
is the momentum coefficient
```

Adam Optimizer

Adam (Adaptive Moment Estimation) is an optimization algorithm that computes adaptive learning rates for each parameter by tracking the first and second moments of the gradients.

The update rules for Adam are as follows:

1. The first moment estimate, representing the mean, is calculated as:

$$m_t = \beta_1 m_{t-1} + (1 - \beta_1)\nabla_\theta L(\theta)$$

2. The second moment estimate, representing the variance, is calculated as:

$$v_t = \beta_2 v_{t-1} + (1 - \beta_2)(\nabla_\theta L(\theta))^2$$

3. The bias correction is performed to adjust for initialization biases in the moments. The corrected first moment is:

$$\hat{m}_t = \frac{m_t}{1-\beta_1^t},$$

and the corrected second moment is:

$$\hat{v}_t = \frac{v_t}{1-\beta_2^t}.$$

The parameter update rule is then applied to adjust the parameters:

$$\theta_{\text{new}} = \theta_{\text{old}} - \eta \frac{\hat{m}_t}{\sqrt{\hat{v}_t}+\epsilon}$$

In these equations, $\beta 1$ and $\beta 2$ are decay rates for the moments, typically set to 0.9 and 0.999, respectively. The constant ϵ is a small value added to prevent division by zero.

There are lots of great things about Adam. It can adapt the learning rate for each parameter, which is really useful. It's also pretty robust even when you don't tweak the settings. And it's really efficient, so it's great for big datasets and complex models.

Following is a quick example:

```
float learningRate = 0.001; // Adam often uses a smaller
learning rate
fl::AdamOptimizer optimizer(params, learningRate);
```

Loss functions and optimization algorithms are what make neural networks learn from data. If you know how different loss functions affect the learning process, you can choose the best one for your task. These tools have been really important in making neural networks better, and they've led to big changes in areas like computer vision, natural language processing, and more.

Using Flashlight's Optimizers

While manually coding backpropagation is educational, in practice, we leverage libraries like Flashlight that provide built-in optimizers and automatic differentiation to simplify the training process. Flashlight's optimizers handle the complexities of gradient computation and parameter updates, allowing us to focus on designing and training our models efficiently.

Flashlight offers several optimizer classes:

1. **`fl::SGDOptimizer`**: Implements Stochastic Gradient Descent.
2. **`fl::AdamOptimizer`**: Implements the Adam optimization algorithm.
3. **`fl::RMSPropOptimizer`**: Implements RMSProp.
4. **`fl::AdagradOptimizer`**: Implements Adagrad.

These optimizers automatically compute gradients during the backward pass and update model parameters.

We will now revisit our training code and see how we can simplify it using Flashlight's optimizers. Here, assuming we have our **SimpleMLP** model defined using Flashlight's modules, we setup the mdel and the loss function:

```
// Define network architecture
SimpleMLP model(inputSize, hiddenSize, outputSize);
// Get model parameters
auto params = model.params();
// Define loss function
auto criterion = fl::CategoricalCrossEntropy();
```

Next, we must choose an optimizer, that can be either SGD or the Adam optimizer. For example, if we use SGD optimizer:

```
float learningRate = 0.01;
fl::SGDOptimizer optimizer(params, learningRate);
```

And, if we prefer to make use of Adam optimizer:

```
float learningRate = 0.001; // Typically smaller learning rate
for Adam
fl::AdamOptimizer optimizer(params, learningRate);
```

Next, it is to train the loop with Flashlight's optimizer. The training loop remains largely the same, but we rely on the optimizer to handle parameter updates.

```
for (int epoch = 1; epoch <= numEpochs; ++epoch) {
    std::cout << "Epoch " << epoch << "/" << numEpochs <<
std::endl;
    int batchIndex = 0;
    float epochLoss = 0.0;
    int correct = 0;
    int total = 0;
    for (auto& batch : *dataLoader) {
```

```
        auto inputs = batch[0];
        auto targets = batch[1];
        // Flatten inputs
        inputs = fl::reshape(inputs, {inputSize, batchSize});
        // Convert to Variables
        fl::Variable inputVar(inputs, false);
        fl::Variable targetVar(targets, false);
        // Forward pass
        auto outputs = model.forward(inputVar);
        // Compute loss
        auto loss = criterion(outputs, targetVar);
        // Backward pass and parameter update
        optimizer.zeroGrad(); // Clear gradients
        loss.backward();      // Compute gradients
        optimizer.step();     // Update parameters
        // Accumulate loss and compute accuracy
        epochLoss += loss.scalar<float>();
        auto predictions = fl::argmax(outputs.tensor(), 0);
        auto targetTensor =
targetVar.tensor().astype(fl::dtype::s32);
        correct += fl::count(predictions ==
targetTensor).asScalar<int>();
        total += batchSize;
        // Print progress
        if (batchIndex % 100 == 0) {
            std::cout << "Batch " << batchIndex << ", Loss: "
<< loss.scalar<float>() << std::endl;
        }
        batchIndex++;
    }
```

```
    // Epoch summary
    float avgLoss = epochLoss / batchIndex;
    float accuracy = static_cast<float>(correct) / total *
100.0f;
    std::cout << "Epoch " << epoch << " completed. Average
Loss: " << avgLoss
              << ", Accuracy: " << accuracy << "%" <<
std::endl;
}
```

Next. We may modify the learning rate over time just to improve convergence. And while we do, we add regularization to prevent overfitting as well.

```
if (epoch % 5 == 0) {
    learningRate *= 0.1;
    optimizer.setLr(learningRate);
}
float weightDecay = 1e-5;
optimizer.setWeightDecay(weightDecay);
// After training loop
model.eval(); // Set model to evaluation mode
float validationAccuracy = evaluate(model,
validationDataLoader);
std::cout << "Validation Accuracy: " << validationAccuracy <<
"%" << std::endl;
```

And the final is to stop training if validation loss stops decreasing.

```
std::string modelPath = "trained_model.bin";
fl::save(modelPath, model);
SimpleMLP model(inputSize, hiddenSize, outputSize);
fl::load(modelPath, model);
```

This not only reduces the amount of code but also minimizes the potential for errors in manual implementations.

Summary

In short, we took a big-picture look at how to train deep neural networks. We started off by taking a close look at the building blocks of a solid training loop, and how important it is to get the epochs, batches, and iterations right. Once we know how these elements affect each other, we can structure our training processes in a way that makes sure models learn from the data as effectively as possible.

We looked at ways to make the training loop more effective, such as data shuffling, learning rate scheduling, and early stopping. These are important for getting the best results and avoiding problems like overfitting. We then learned about how loss functions and optimization algorithms are really important. We looked at some common loss functions, like cross-entropy and mean squared error, and saw how they direct the learning process by measuring how well the model is doing. We also looked at different optimization algorithms, like Stochastic Gradient Descent (SGD) and Adam. We saw how they adjust model parameters to minimize the loss function.

Finally, we manually implemented backpropagation to gain a deeper understanding of how gradients are computed. We also demonstrated how Flashlight's built-in optimizers can simplify the training process, allowing us to focus more on model design and less on the underlying computations.

CHAPTER 5: CONVOLUTIONAL NEURAL NETWORKS (CNNs)

Chapter Overview

In this chapter, we will take a deep dive into convolutional neural networks (CNNs). They've transformed the field of computer vision. We will start by looking at what CNNs are and how they're different from traditional neural networks. Knowing how convolutional layers, pooling layers, and activation functions work will help us understand how CNNs process spatial data effectively.

Next, we will look at implementing convolutional layers. We will see how to apply filters to input data to extract meaningful features. With that in mind, we will put together a CNN model that's tailored for image classification tasks, using the Flashlight library to its fullest. Once we've built the model, we will train our CNN using the CIFAR-10 dataset, using the techniques and strategies we've learned previously. Then, we will evaluate the model's performance, looking at metrics like accuracy and loss, and learn about ways to improve it further.

By the end of this chapter, You will have a good understanding of CNNs and some experience of building and training them for image processing tasks.

Introduction to CNNs

Convolutional Neural Networks (CNNs) are a specialized class of neural networks designed to process data with a grid-like topology, such as images. Unlike traditional feedforward neural networks that treat inputs as a one-dimensional array, CNNs take advantage of the spatial structure of data. They are particularly effective in handling image data because they can capture spatial hierarchies and patterns through the use of convolutional layers.

Key Components of CNNs

Convolutional Layers

The convolutional layer is the core building block of a CNN. It applies a set of learnable filters (also known as kernels) to the input data. Each filter convolves across the input image, computing dot products to produce a feature map that represents the presence of specific features in the input.

- **Filters/Kernels**: Small matrices that slide over the input data to detect patterns.
- **Feature Maps**: The output of the convolution operation, highlighting the presence of features detected by the filters.
- **Stride**: The number of pixels by which the filter moves over the input matrix.
- **Padding**: Adding zeros around the input matrix borders to control the spatial size of the output feature maps.

Activation Functions

Non-linear activation functions are applied after convolutional layers to introduce non-linearity into the network, enabling it to learn complex patterns. The most commonly used activation function in CNNs is the Rectified Linear Unit (ReLU), defined as:

$$ReLU(x) = max(0, x)$$

ReLU activation helps in mitigating the vanishing gradient problem and accelerates the convergence of the network.

Pooling Layers

Pooling layers reduce the spatial dimensions of the feature maps, which helps in decreasing computational complexity and controlling overfitting.

- **Max Pooling**: Selects the maximum value from a region of the feature map.
- **Average Pooling**: Computes the average value within a region.

Pooling layers summarize the presence of features in a region, providing spatial variance and making the detection of features more robust.

Fully Connected Layers

After several convolutional and pooling layers, the high-level reasoning in the neural network is performed via fully connected layers. These layers interpret the features extracted by previous layers and output the final classification.

How CNNs Work?

CNNs operate by processing input data through a sequence of layers, with each layer designed to extract increasingly intricate features from the data. This process can be broadly categorized into two main stages: feature extraction and classification.

In the feature extraction stage, the early layers of a CNN focus on detecting fundamental elements of the input, such as edges and textures. These initial filters capture basic spatial patterns that serve as building blocks for understanding more complex structures. Moving deeper into the network, the intermediate layers begin to identify more sophisticated patterns, such as specific shapes or parts of objects. These layers build upon the foundational features identified earlier to form a more detailed understanding of the input data. Finally, the deepest layers of the CNN specialize in recognizing high-level concepts, such as entire objects or faces, by combining the detailed patterns detected in preceding layers.

The classification stage begins with a process called flattening, where the final set of feature maps generated during feature extraction is transformed into a one-dimensional vector. This transformation allows the network to handle the data in a format suitable for classification tasks.

Following flattening, fully connected layers are employed to process this vector and assign the input data to a specific category or class. These layers use the high-level features extracted in earlier stages to make predictions about the data, completing the overall workflow of a CNN.

Developments and Contributions of CNNs

One of the earliest architectures, LeNet-5, introduced by Yann LeCun in 1998, laid the foundation for CNNs. It was designed primarily for handwritten digit recognition and effectively demonstrated the potential of CNNs in processing image data. Following this, AlexNet, introduced in 2012, revolutionized the field by winning the ImageNet Large Scale Visual Recognition Challenge (ILSVRC). This architecture utilized deeper networks and GPU acceleration to achieve remarkable accuracy, reducing the top-5 error rate from 26% to 15%, thus showcasing the power of deeper architectures and hardware advancements.

The next significant contribution came from VGGNet in 2014, which emphasized the importance of network depth for improved performance. By using very small convolutional filters (3x3) and increasing the network depth up to 19 layers, VGGNet demonstrated that deeper networks could lead to superior results in image classification tasks. That same year, GoogLeNet, featuring the innovative Inception module, was introduced. The Inception module allowed filters of multiple sizes to operate in parallel, enabling more efficient computation while maintaining high performance. This innovation reduced computational costs significantly.

In 2015, ResNet took CNN development to another level by introducing residual learning. This technique addressed the vanishing gradient problem, enabling networks to achieve unprecedented depth—over 100 layers. ResNet's success was marked by its victory in the ILSVRC 2015 challenge, where it set new benchmarks for image classification accuracy. Collectively, these developments have established CNNs as a cornerstone of modern computer vision.

Applications of CNNs

CNNs have found diverse applications across numerous domains, transforming industries with their capabilities. Image classification is one of the fundamental applications, where CNNs are used to assign labels to images, such as identifying whether an image contains a cat or a dog. In object detection, CNNs go further by not only identifying objects in an image but also localizing them, a critical function in fields like autonomous driving and surveillance.

Another important application is image segmentation, where CNNs partition an image into meaningful segments to identify boundaries and objects. This technique is widely used in medical imaging for precise analysis and scene understanding in robotics. Face recognition, another major application, involves identifying or verifying a person from a digital image and has become a staple in security systems and social media platforms. Additionally, CNNs are employed in style transfer, an artistic application where the style of one image is applied to another, blending content and style to produce creative outputs.

CNNs are particularly well-suited for processing image data due to several inherent advantages.

First, they enable efficient computation by using convolution operations that are computationally less intensive than fully connected layers, especially when dealing with large images. Additionally, CNNs offer automatic feature extraction, learning optimal filters for feature extraction directly from the data and eliminating the need for manual feature engineering. This adaptability enhances their utility across various applications.

Another key advantage of CNNs is their ability to achieve better generalization. Features like parameter sharing and local connectivity help CNNs generalize well to new data, ensuring reliable performance in real-world scenarios. These characteristics make CNNs not only powerful but also versatile, cementing their place as the preferred choice for image-related tasks in machine learning.

Implement Convolutional Layers

In the previous chapters, we built a MLP using fully connected layers to classify images from the CIFAR-10 dataset. While MLPs can handle small-scale problems, they are not well-suited for image data because they do not capture the spatial hierarchy of images. To address this, we will introduce convolutional layers into our neural network using the Flashlight library, enhancing the model's ability to recognize patterns and features in images.

The primary class for convolutional layers is **fl::Conv2D**, which applies a 2D convolution over an input signal composed of several input planes.

Following are the key parameters of **fl::Conv2D**:

- **`inChannels`**: Number of channels in the input image.
- **`outChannels`**: Number of filters (kernels) and the number of output channels.
- **`kernelHeight` and `kernelWidth`**: Dimensions of the convolutional kernel.
- **`strideHeight` and `strideWidth`**: Stride of the convolution along height and width.
- **`paddingHeight` and `paddingWidth`**: Implicit zero paddings on both sides of the input.
- **`groups`**: Number of blocked connections from input channels to output channels.

Add Convolutional Layers to Neural Network Model

We will modify our existing **SimpleMLP** class by creating a new class **SimpleCNN** that incorporates convolutional layers. We will use the **fl::Sequential** container to stack layers sequentially.

- Create a New Header File: **`simple_cnn.h`**

```
#ifndef SIMPLE_CNN_H
#define SIMPLE_CNN_H
#include <flashlight/flashlight.h>
class SimpleCNN : public fl::Sequential {
public:
    SimpleCNN();
};
#endif // SIMPLE_CNN_H
```

- Implement the Convolutional Layers in **simple_cnn.cpp**

```
#include "simple_cnn.h"
SimpleCNN::SimpleCNN() {
    // Input shape: [Channels, Height, Width, BatchSize]
    // CIFAR-10 images are 32x32 with 3 channels
    // First Convolutional Layer
    add(fl::Conv2D(3, 16, 3, 3, 1, 1, 1, 1)); // inChannels=3,
outChannels=16, kernel=3x3, stride=1x1, padding=1x1
    add(fl::ReLU());
    add(fl::MaxPool2D(2, 2, 2, 2)); // kernel=2x2, stride=2x2
    // Second Convolutional Layer
    add(fl::Conv2D(16, 32, 3, 3, 1, 1, 1, 1));
    add(fl::ReLU());
    add(fl::MaxPool2D(2, 2, 2, 2));
    // Third Convolutional Layer
    add(fl::Conv2D(32, 64, 3, 3, 1, 1, 1, 1));
    add(fl::ReLU());
    add(fl::MaxPool2D(2, 2, 2, 2));
    // Flatten the tensor
    add(fl::View({-1, 0, 0, 0})); // Flatten all dimensions
except batch size
```

```
    // Fully Connected Layers
    add(fl::Linear(64 * 4 * 4, 128));
    add(fl::ReLU());
    add(fl::Dropout(0.5));
    add(fl::Linear(128, 10)); // CIFAR-10 has 10 classes
    add(fl::LogSoftmax());
}
```

The architecture described above begins with the first convolutional layer, which takes input channels corresponding to the three RGB color channels of an image. This layer produces 16 output channels by applying a 3x3 kernel with a stride of 1x1 and padding of 1x1, ensuring the resulting feature map retains a size of 32x32. A max-pooling operation is applied afterward, reducing the spatial dimensions of the feature map to 16x16.

Following this, the second convolutional layer processes the 16 input channels from the previous layer, generating 32 output channels. After applying max pooling, the resulting feature map size is further reduced to 8x8. The architecture then proceeds to the third convolutional layer, which takes the 32 input channels from the prior layer and outputs 64 channels. The max-pooling operation applied here results in a final feature map size of 4x4.

Subsequently, the architecture includes a flattening layer that transforms the 64 feature maps, each of size 4x4, into a single one-dimensional vector. This process results in a flattened vector of 1024 elements (64 * 4 * 4). The fully connected layers then handle this flattened data. The first fully connected (FC) layer maps the 1024 inputs to 128 neurons, effectively reducing the dimensionality. Finally, the second fully connected layer maps the 128 inputs to 10 outputs, corresponding to the number of target classes in the classification task.

Update Training Code

In **main.cpp**, we will use the new **SimpleCNN** model.

```
#include "simple_cnn.h"
```

We then modify the model initialization:

```
// Initialize the CNN model
SimpleCNN model;
// Get model parameters
auto params = model.params();
```

```
// Define loss function and optimizer
auto criterion = fl::NegativeLogLikelihood();
float learningRate = 0.001;
fl::AdamOptimizer optimizer(params, learningRate);
```

Since convolutional layers preserve the spatial dimensions, we no longer need to flatten the input images.

```
for (auto& batch : *dataLoader) {
    auto inputs = batch[0];  // Batch of images with shape [3,
32, 32, batchSize]
    auto targets = batch[1]; // Batch of labels
    // Convert inputs and targets to Variables
    fl::Variable inputVar(inputs, false);
    fl::Variable targetVar(targets, false);
    // Forward pass
    auto outputs = model.forward(inputVar);
    // Compute loss and perform backward pass
    auto loss = criterion(outputs, targetVar);
    optimizer.zeroGrad();
    loss.backward();
    optimizer.step();
    // ... (Rest of the training loop)
}
```

Compiling and Running Model

Add **simple_cnn.cpp** to the list of source files.

```
add_executable(ml_project
    src/main.cpp
    src/cifar10_loader.cpp
    src/cifar10_dataset.cpp
```

```
    src/simple_cnn.cpp
)
```

Then, compile and run:

```
cd ~/ml_project/build
cmake ..
make
./ml_project
```

Here in the above demonstration, we've reduced the learning rate to 0.001 since Adam optimizer often performs better with smaller learning rates. We also have to ensure that the batch size is appropriate for your hardware to avoid out-of-memory errors.

Building CNN Model for CIFAR-10

Now that we've implemented convolutional layers, we will build a complete CNN model tailored for image classification using the CIFAR-10 dataset. We will construct a deeper network that can capture intricate patterns in the images to improve classification accuracy.

To ease the understanding, we will design a CNN model with the following architecture:

1. **Convolutional Block 1, Block 2 and Block 3:**
    - Conv2D layer
    - Batch Normalization
    - ReLU activation
    - Max Pooling
2. **Fully Connected Layers:**
    - Flatten layer
    - Dense layer with ReLU and Dropout
    - Output layer with LogSoftmax

Implementing CNN Model

To begin with, we will make sure that the header file includes any new modules used.

```
#ifndef SIMPLE_CNN_H
```

```
#define SIMPLE_CNN_H
#include <flashlight/flashlight.h>
class SimpleCNN : public fl::Sequential {
public:
    SimpleCNN();
};
#endif // SIMPLE_CNN_H
```

Next, we simply implement the CNN in **simple_cnn.cpp**:

```
#include "simple_cnn.h"
SimpleCNN::SimpleCNN() {
    // Convolutional Block 1
    add(fl::Conv2D(3, 32, 3, 3, 1, 1, 1, 1)); // inChannels=3,
outChannels=32
    add(fl::BatchNorm(32));
    add(fl::ReLU());
    add(fl::MaxPool2D(2, 2, 2, 2));
    // Convolutional Block 2
    add(fl::Conv2D(32, 64, 3, 3, 1, 1, 1, 1));
    add(fl::BatchNorm(64));
    add(fl::ReLU());
    add(fl::MaxPool2D(2, 2, 2, 2));
    // Convolutional Block 3
    add(fl::Conv2D(64, 128, 3, 3, 1, 1, 1, 1));
    add(fl::BatchNorm(128));
    add(fl::ReLU());
    add(fl::MaxPool2D(2, 2, 2, 2));
    // Flatten the tensor
    add(fl::View({-1, 0, 0, 0}));
```

```
    // Fully Connected Layers
    add(fl::Linear(128 * 4 * 4, 256));
    add(fl::ReLU());
    add(fl::Dropout(0.5));
    add(fl::Linear(256, 10)); // CIFAR-10 classes
    add(fl::LogSoftmax());
}
```

Next, in the **main.cpp**, we check the batch size and learning rate are appropriate by modifying the optimizer initialization:

```
float learningRate = 0.001;
fl::AdamOptimizer optimizer(model.params(), learningRate);
```

If we have sufficient computational resources, we can think of considering to increase the number of epochs.

```
int numEpochs = 20; // Increase epochs for better training
```

Next, to evaluate the model's performance during training, we will include a validation set.

Now, assuming **dataset** contains all the training data, we will split it.

```
// Assuming dataset is a vector of samples
size_t validationSize = dataset.size() * 0.1; // 10% for
validation
std::vector<std::tuple<fl::Tensor, int>>
trainData(dataset.begin(), dataset.end() - validationSize);
std::vector<std::tuple<fl::Tensor, int>> valData(dataset.end()
- validationSize, dataset.end());
```

We then, create data loaders for training and validation:

```
// Training Data Loader
CIFAR10Dataset trainDataset(trainData, true);
auto trainBatchDataset = fl::BatchDataset(
    std::make_shared<CIFAR10Dataset>(trainDataset),
```

```
    batchSize
);
auto trainDataLoader = fl::PrefetchDataset(trainBatchDataset,
4);
// Validation Data Loader
CIFAR10Dataset valDataset(valData, false);
auto valBatchDataset = fl::BatchDataset(
    std::make_shared<CIFAR10Dataset>(valDataset),
    batchSize
);
auto valDataLoader = fl::PrefetchDataset(valBatchDataset, 4);
```

Next, we modify the training loop to include validation:

```
for (int epoch = 1; epoch <= numEpochs; ++epoch) {
    // Training phase
    model.train(); // Set model to training mode
    float trainLoss = 0.0;
    int correctTrain = 0;
    int totalTrain = 0;
    for (auto& batch : *trainDataLoader) {
        // Training code as before
    }
    // Validation phase
    model.eval(); // Set model to evaluation mode
    float valLoss = 0.0;
    int correctVal = 0;
    int totalVal = 0;
    for (auto& batch : *valDataLoader) {
        auto inputs = batch[0];
        auto targets = batch[1];
```

```
        fl::Variable inputVar(inputs, false);
        fl::Variable targetVar(targets, false);
        // Forward pass
        auto outputs = model.forward(inputVar);
        auto loss = criterion(outputs, targetVar);
        valLoss += loss.scalar<float>();
        // Compute accuracy
        auto predictions = fl::argmax(outputs.tensor(), 0);
        auto targetTensor =
targetVar.tensor().astype(fl::dtype::s32);
        correctVal += fl::count(predictions ==
targetTensor).asScalar<int>();
        totalVal += batchSize;
    }
    // Calculate average losses and accuracies
    float avgTrainLoss = trainLoss / trainBatchDataset.size();
    float trainAccuracy = static_cast<float>(correctTrain) /
totalTrain * 100.0f;
    float avgValLoss = valLoss / valBatchDataset.size();
    float valAccuracy = static_cast<float>(correctVal) /
totalVal * 100.0f;
    std::cout << "Epoch [" << epoch << "/" << numEpochs << "]
"
              << "Train Loss: " << avgTrainLoss << ", Train
Acc: " << trainAccuracy << "%, "
              << "Val Loss: " << avgValLoss << ", Val Acc: "
<< valAccuracy << "%" << std::endl;
}
```

Implementing Early Stopping

To prevent overfitting, we can implement early stopping based on validation loss.

```
float bestValLoss = std::numeric_limits<float>::max();
int epochsNoImprovement = 0;
int patience = 5; // Number of epochs to wait before stopping
if (avgValLoss < bestValLoss) {
    bestValLoss = avgValLoss;
    epochsNoImprovement = 0;
    // Save the best model
    fl::save("best_model.bin", model);
} else {
    epochsNoImprovement++;
    if (epochsNoImprovement >= patience) {
        std::cout << "Early stopping triggered." << std::endl;
        break;
    }
}
```

Evaluating Model Performance

After training, we can evaluate the model on the test set as below:

```
CIFAR10Loader testLoader(dataDir, false);
auto testDatasetData = testLoader.getData();
CIFAR10Dataset testDataset(testDatasetData, false);
auto testBatchDataset = fl::BatchDataset(
    std::make_shared<CIFAR10Dataset>(testDataset),
    batchSize
);
auto testDataLoader = fl::PrefetchDataset(testBatchDataset,
4);
```

Following is the evaluation loop:

```
model.eval();
```

```
float testLoss = 0.0;
int correctTest = 0;
int totalTest = 0;
for (auto& batch : *testDataLoader) {
    auto inputs = batch[0];
    auto targets = batch[1];
    fl::Variable inputVar(inputs, false);
    fl::Variable targetVar(targets, false);
    auto outputs = model.forward(inputVar);
    auto loss = criterion(outputs, targetVar);
    testLoss += loss.scalar<float>();
    auto predictions = fl::argmax(outputs.tensor(), 0);
    auto targetTensor =
targetVar.tensor().astype(fl::dtype::s32);
    correctTest += fl::count(predictions ==
targetTensor).asScalar<int>();
    totalTest += batchSize;
}
float avgTestLoss = testLoss / testBatchDataset.size();
float testAccuracy = static_cast<float>(correctTest) /
totalTest * 100.0f;
std::cout << "Test Loss: " << avgTestLoss << ", Test Accuracy:
" << testAccuracy << "%" << std::endl;
```

This hands-on exercise showed how convolutional layers extract spatial features and how pooling layers reduce dimensionality, which contributes to a better image classification model. Next, We will look at training the CNN model, checking how well it's doing, and exploring ways to make it even better.

Training CNN Model

Now that we've built and tested our CNN model, let's start training it on the CIFAR-10 dataset. You have to feed the network with training data, compute the loss, perform backpropagation to update the weights, and then go through multiple epochs of this. We will use the training loop we talked about in previous chapters, making the necessary adjustments for our CNN.

Prepare Training Environment

At first, we set the hyperparameters to begin with the training:

```
int numEpochs = 20;              // Number of epochs to train
int batchSize = 64;              // Batch size for training
float learningRate = 0.001;      // Learning rate for the
optimizer
```

Since, we have already set up the data loaders for training, validation, and testing in the previous section, we now just simply ensure that the data loaders are properly configured.

Next, we then initialize the model, loss function, and optimizer as below:

```
// Initialize the CNN model
SimpleCNN model;
// Define loss function and optimizer
auto criterion = fl::NegativeLogLikelihood();
fl::AdamOptimizer optimizer(model.params(), learningRate);
```

In addition, if we have a GPU available, we can move the model and data to the GPU for faster training:

```
// Check if CUDA is available
if (fl::cuda::isAvailable()) {
    fl::setDevice(0); // Set device to GPU 0
    model.to(fl::dtype::f32, /* copy */ false,
fl::MemoryLocation::CUDA);
}
```

Training Loop

In order to implement the training loop, we first incorporate the training and validation phases:

```
for (int epoch = 1; epoch <= numEpochs; ++epoch) {
    // ===== Training Phase =====
```

```
    model.train(); // Set model to training mode
    float trainLoss = 0.0;
    int correctTrain = 0;
    int totalTrain = 0;
    int batchIndex = 0;
    for (auto& batch : *trainDataLoader) {
        auto inputs = batch[0];
        auto targets = batch[1];
        // Move data to GPU if available
        if (fl::cuda::isAvailable()) {
            inputs = inputs.to(fl::dtype::f32,
fl::MemoryLocation::CUDA);
            targets = targets.to(fl::dtype::s32,
fl::MemoryLocation::CUDA);
        }
        // Convert to Variables
        fl::Variable inputVar(inputs, false);
        fl::Variable targetVar(targets, false);
        // Forward pass
        auto outputs = model.forward(inputVar);
        // Compute loss
        auto loss = criterion(outputs, targetVar);
        // Backward pass and optimization
        optimizer.zeroGrad();
        loss.backward();
        optimizer.step();
        // Accumulate training loss
        trainLoss += loss.scalar<float>();
        // Compute training accuracy
        auto predictions = fl::argmax(outputs.tensor(), 0);
```

```
        auto targetTensor =
targetVar.tensor().astype(fl::dtype::s32);
        correctTrain += fl::count(predictions ==
targetTensor).asScalar<int>();
        totalTrain += batchSize;
        // Print training progress every 100 batches
        if (batchIndex % 100 == 0) {
            std::cout << "Epoch [" << epoch << "/" <<
numEpochs << "], Batch [" << batchIndex
                      << "], Loss: " << loss.scalar<float>()
<< std::endl;
        }
        batchIndex++;
    }
    // Calculate average training loss and accuracy
    float avgTrainLoss = trainLoss / batchIndex;
    float trainAccuracy = static_cast<float>(correctTrain) /
totalTrain * 100.0f;
    // ===== Validation Phase =====
    model.eval(); // Set model to evaluation mode
    float valLoss = 0.0;
    int correctVal = 0;
    int totalVal = 0;
    batchIndex = 0;
    for (auto& batch : *valDataLoader) {
        auto inputs = batch[0];
        auto targets = batch[1];
        if (fl::cuda::isAvailable()) {
            inputs = inputs.to(fl::dtype::f32,
fl::MemoryLocation::CUDA);
```

```
            targets = targets.to(fl::dtype::s32,
fl::MemoryLocation::CUDA);
        }
        fl::Variable inputVar(inputs, false);
        fl::Variable targetVar(targets, false);
        // Forward pass (no gradient computation needed)
        auto outputs = model.forward(inputVar);
        auto loss = criterion(outputs, targetVar);
        valLoss += loss.scalar<float>();
        // Compute validation accuracy
        auto predictions = fl::argmax(outputs.tensor(), 0);
        auto targetTensor =
targetVar.tensor().astype(fl::dtype::s32);
        correctVal += fl::count(predictions ==
targetTensor).asScalar<int>();
        totalVal += batchSize;
        batchIndex++;
    }
    // Calculate average validation loss and accuracy
    float avgValLoss = valLoss / batchIndex;
    float valAccuracy = static_cast<float>(correctVal) /
totalVal * 100.0f;
    // Print epoch summary
    std::cout << "Epoch [" << epoch << "/" << numEpochs << "]
"
              << "Train Loss: " << avgTrainLoss << ", Train
Acc: " << trainAccuracy << "%, "
              << "Val Loss: " << avgValLoss << ", Val Acc: "
<< valAccuracy << "%" << std::endl;
    // Implement early stopping or save the best model if
needed
```

```
}
```

Now in the above Training Phase,

- The model is explicitly set to training mode using **`model.train()`**. It enables training-specific behaviors like dropout layers and batch normalization to function correctly. These layers behave differently during training versus evaluation, ensuring the model learns properly.
- The predictions from the model are compared to the actual target labels using a loss function, such as **`CrossEntropyLoss`** or **`Mean Squared Error`**.
- Backpropagation is performed by computing gradients of the loss with respect to the model's parameters using **`loss.backward()`**.

And in the Validation Phase,

- Gradients are not computed to save computation resources. This is achieved by wrapping the validation loop with **`torch.no_grad()`**.
- The model's predictions are evaluated on the validation dataset using the same loss function as in training to monitor how well it is generalizing to unseen data.
- Additional metrics like accuracy, precision, recall, or F1 score may be computed to gain a comprehensive view of the model's validation performance.

After training, simply save the model for future use:

```
fl::save("cnn_cifar10_model.bin", model);
```

Evaluating Model Performance

We will now move on to assess the model's accuracy on the test dataset and explore additional evaluation metrics.

At first, we will load the model which we saved during training in the previous section.

```
SimpleCNN model;
fl::load("cnn_cifar10_model.bin", model);
```

Next, we set the model to evaluation mode as shown below:

```
model.eval(); // Disable dropout and batch normalization
updates
```

Next is the evaluation loop:

```
float testLoss = 0.0;
int correctTest = 0;
int totalTest = 0;
int batchIndex = 0;
for (auto& batch : *testDataLoader) {
    auto inputs = batch[0];
    auto targets = batch[1];
    if (fl::cuda::isAvailable()) {
        inputs = inputs.to(fl::dtype::f32,
fl::MemoryLocation::CUDA);
        targets = targets.to(fl::dtype::s32,
fl::MemoryLocation::CUDA);
    }
    fl::Variable inputVar(inputs, false);
    fl::Variable targetVar(targets, false);
    // Forward pass
    auto outputs = model.forward(inputVar);
    auto loss = criterion(outputs, targetVar);
    testLoss += loss.scalar<float>();
    // Compute accuracy
    auto predictions = fl::argmax(outputs.tensor(), 0);
    auto targetTensor =
targetVar.tensor().astype(fl::dtype::s32);
    correctTest += fl::count(predictions ==
targetTensor).asScalar<int>();
    totalTest += batchSize;
    batchIndex++;
}
// Calculate average test loss and accuracy
```

```
float avgTestLoss = testLoss / batchIndex;

float testAccuracy = static_cast<float>(correctTest) /
totalTest * 100.0f;

std::cout << "Test Loss: " << avgTestLoss << ", Test Accuracy:
" << testAccuracy << "%" << std::endl;
```

Here, we don't need to compute gradients during evaluation, and it also saves computation time. We then compare the predicted classes with the actual labels to compute the overall accuracy.

If the test accuracy is close to the validation accuracy, it indicates good generalization.

Let us consider the below as a sample output:

```
Test Loss: 0.780, Test Accuracy: 74.5%
```

Here also even if the accuracy is a useful metric, it doesn't provide a complete picture of the model's performance. For this, we can consider the following additional metrics:

- Confusion Matrix

A confusion matrix provides detailed insights into the model's performance by showing the number of correct and incorrect predictions for each class.

See the following implementation:

```
#include <array>

const int numClasses = 10;

std::array<std::array<int, numClasses>, numClasses>
confusionMatrix = {};

for (auto& batch : *testDataLoader) {

    // ... (Same as evaluation loop)

    auto predictions = fl::argmax(outputs.tensor(), 0);

    auto targetTensor =
targetVar.tensor().astype(fl::dtype::s32);

    for (int i = 0; i < batchSize; ++i) {

        int actual = targetTensor(i).asScalar<int>();

        int predicted = predictions(i).asScalar<int>();

        confusionMatrix[actual][predicted]++;

    }
```

```
}
// Display confusion matrix
std::cout << "Confusion Matrix:\n";
for (int i = 0; i < numClasses; ++i) {
    for (int j = 0; j < numClasses; ++j) {
        std::cout << confusionMatrix[i][j] << " ";
    }
    std::cout << std::endl;
}
```

- Classification Report

This thing computes precision, recall, and F1-score for each class. To implement, you would need to count true positives, false positives, and false negatives for each class.

- Top-5 Accuracy

In some applications, it's acceptable if the correct class is among the top 5 predictions. Check the below implementation to understand it better practically:

```
int top5Correct = 0;
for (auto& batch : *testDataLoader) {
    // ... (Same as evaluation loop)
    auto outputsTensor = outputs.tensor();
    auto targetTensor =
targetVar.tensor().astype(fl::dtype::s32);
    for (int i = 0; i < batchSize; ++i) {
        auto probs = outputsTensor(fl::span, i);
        auto topKIndices = fl::topk(probs, 5);
        int actual = targetTensor(i).asScalar<int>();
        for (int k = 0; k < 5; ++k) {
            if (topKIndices.indices(k).asScalar<int>() ==
actual) {
                top5Correct++;
```

```
                    break;
                }
            }
        }
    }
float top5Accuracy = static_cast<float>(top5Correct) /
totalTest * 100.0f;
std::cout << "Top-5 Test Accuracy: " << top5Accuracy << "%" <<
std::endl;
```

- Visualizing Predictions

The visualization of test images along with their predicted and actual labels can also provide qualitative insights. See the following implementation:

```
#include <matplotlibcpp.h>
namespace plt = matplotlibcpp;
// Assume batchSize is set to 1 for simplicity
auto batch = testDataLoader->get(0);
auto inputs = batch[0];
auto targets = batch[1];
if (fl::cuda::isAvailable()) {
    inputs = inputs.to(fl::dtype::f32,
fl::MemoryLocation::CUDA);
}
fl::Variable inputVar(inputs, false);
auto outputs = model.forward(inputVar);
auto predictions = fl::argmax(outputs.tensor(), 0);
int actualLabel = targets(0).asScalar<int>();
int predictedLabel = predictions(0).asScalar<int>();
// Convert tensor to image
auto imageTensor = inputs(fl::span, fl::span, fl::span,
0).toHost();
```

```
std::vector<uint8_t> imageData(imageTensor.elements());
std::copy(imageTensor.host<uint8_t>(),
imageTensor.host<uint8_t>() + imageTensor.elements(),
imageData.begin());
// Reshape and display image
plt::imshow(imageData, 32, 32, 3);
plt::title("Actual: " + std::to_string(actualLabel) + ",
Predicted: " + std::to_string(predictedLabel));
plt::show();
```

To sum up, how well a model works depends on lots of different things. If you look at it in detail with various ways of showing what's wrong or right with it, You will understand it better and be able to make changes that'll make it even better.

Summary

Overall, we looked at how CNNs are making a big splash in image processing tasks. We started by taking a look at the building blocks of CNNs, including convolutional layers, pooling layers, activation functions, and fully connected layers. These parts work together to find patterns and hierarchies in image data, which makes CNNs really effective for tasks like image classification.

Next, we added convolutional layers using the Flashlight library, which made our neural network better at handling image data. Building on this, we put together a CNN model that's tailored to the CIFAR-10 dataset. We added layers like batch normalization and dropout to improve performance and prevent overfitting. We trained the CNN model and saw a big improvement in accuracy compared to our previous MLP model. Finally, we evaluated the model's performance using various metrics, which gave us insights into its strengths and areas for further improvement.

Chapter 6: Improving Model Performance

Chapter Overview

In this chapter, we will look at ways to make our neural network models perform better and generalise better. We will start by looking at overfitting, which is when a model does well on the training data but doesn't do so well on the unseen data. We will look at ways to stop overfitting, including regularization methods.

Next, we will look at how to use dropout and batch normalization to reduce overfitting and speed up training. We will also look at more sophisticated ways to expand our data set and help the model become more reliable. We will learn about tuning hyperparameters, including things like learning rates, batch sizes, and network architectures, to help get better results. We will also look at how to analyze and interpret results, so you can make informed decisions based on model evaluations and visualizations. After this chapter, You will have a range of techniques to improve and enhance your models.

Preventing Overfitting

Overfitting is a critical challenge in machine learning where a model learns not only the underlying patterns in the training data but also the noise and outliers. This results in a model that performs exceptionally well on training data but fails to generalize to new, unseen data. The issue of overfitting became prominent with the rise of complex models, such as deep neural networks, which have a high capacity to fit data.

As machine learning models grew in complexity, they required mechanisms to ensure they could generalize beyond the training dataset. Early instances of overfitting were observed in models like decision trees and polynomial regression, but the problem became more acute with deep learning due to the large number of parameters involved. Understanding and preventing overfitting is essential to developing reliable models that perform well in real-world scenarios.

Understanding Overfitting

Overfitting occurs when a model captures the noise along with the underlying pattern in the data. It essentially memorizes the training data, including the random fluctuations and outliers, rather than learning the general trend.

Following are the indicators of overfitting:

- **High Training Accuracy but Low Validation/Test Accuracy:** The model performs extremely well on training data but poorly on validation or test data.
- **Diverging Loss Curves:** Training loss decreases while validation loss starts increasing after a certain point.

- **Complexity without Improvement:** Adding more layers or parameters doesn't improve validation performance.

Given below are the causes of overfitting:

- Models with more parameters than necessary can fit the training data too closely.
- Not enough data to capture the true distribution, leading the model to learn noise.
- Presence of outliers or errors in the training data.
- No constraints on the model's ability to fit the training data.

Regularization for Overfitting

One thing regularization does is add a penalty for more complex models to discourage them from fitting noise in the training data, which is a good thing.

- L1 Regularization (Lasso):

L1 Regularization, also called Lasso, adds the absolute value of the magnitude of coefficients as a penalty term to the loss function.

$$\text{Loss}_{\text{total}} = \text{Loss}_{\text{original}} + \lambda \sum_{i=1}^{n} |w_i|$$

It encourages sparsity, thereby leading some weights to become zero, effectively removing less important features.

- L2 Regularization (Ridge):

It adds the squared magnitude of coefficients as a penalty term. This penalizes large weights, which helps to smooth out the model and prevent extreme values.

$$\text{Loss}_{\text{total}} = \text{Loss}_{\text{original}} + \lambda \sum_{i=1}^{n} w_i^2$$

When it comes to choosing a regularization parameter (λ), there are a couple of things to keep in mind. First, it's all about striking a balance between fitting the training data and keeping the model weights small. And second, it's not a one-size-fits-all situation. So You will need to tune it to get the best results.

Implementing L2 Regularization

Coming back to Flashlight, you need to add weight decay to the optimizer, which acts as L2 regularization.

```
float weightDecay = 1e-4; // Regularization strength
fl::AdamOptimizer optimizer(model.params(), learningRate);
optimizer.setWeightDecay(weightDecay);
```

Next, keep monitoring the validation loss. You may stop training once you find it has stopped improving.

```
float bestValLoss = std::numeric_limits<float>::max();
int patience = 5;
int epochsNoImprovement = 0;
for (int epoch = 1; epoch <= numEpochs; ++epoch) {
    // Training and validation code...
    if (avgValLoss < bestValLoss) {
        bestValLoss = avgValLoss;
        epochsNoImprovement = 0;
        // Save the best model
        fl::save("best_model.bin", model);
    } else {
        epochsNoImprovement++;
        if (epochsNoImprovement >= patience) {
            std::cout << "Early stopping triggered at epoch "
<< epoch << std::endl;
            break;
        }
    }
}
```

You may also enhance your **CIFAR10Dataset** class to include data augmentation techniques.

Implementing Dropout and Batch Normalization

Understanding Dropout

In machine learning, dropout is a regularization technique that randomly sets a fraction of neurons to zero during the training phase. This makes sure the network doesn't get too reliant on any particular neuron, which helps it develop redundant representations. This helps to reduce overfitting and improve the model's ability to generalise.

Let us see how dropout works? Infact during training,

- Each neuron has a chance, or probability, of being kept (not dropped) at p.
- The outputs of the neurons that were dropped are multiplied by zero, which effectively removes them from the network for that iteration.
- The remaining neurons are scaled by $p1$ to keep the overall output the same. During inference, dropout is disabled and all neurons are active. There's no scaling because the network has learned to be robust to missing neurons during training.

Now, there are also couple of key benefits to dropout:

- First, it helps to prevent overfitting. This is because it stops neurons from adapting to each other.
- Another benefit is that it encourages the network to learn features that are robust. This means it learns features that are useful even if the random subsets of neurons change a lot.

Understanding Batch Normalization

Batch Normalization (BatchNorm) is a technique that normalizes the inputs of each layer to have zero mean and unit variance. It addresses the problem of internal covariate shift, where the distribution of inputs to a layer changes during training, slowing down the learning process.

To apply normalization, first for each mini-batch, compute the mean μ and variance σ^2 of the inputs. Then, normalize the inputs:

$$\hat{x} = \frac{x-\mu}{\sqrt{\sigma^2+\epsilon}}$$

Next, apply learned parameters γ(scale) and β(shift): $y = \gamma x^\wedge + \beta y$. And then use the running averages of μ and σ^2 computed during training.

Incorporate Dropout and Batch Normalization

We will enhance our existing **SimpleCNN** model by adding dropout layers after certain layers and applying batch normalization to the outputs of convolutional layers.

To begin with, we make sure that the header file includes necessary headers:

```
#ifndef SIMPLE_CNN_H
#define SIMPLE_CNN_H
#include <flashlight/flashlight.h>
class SimpleCNN : public fl::Sequential {
public:
    SimpleCNN();
};
#endif // SIMPLE_CNN_H
```

Next, we are modifying **simple_cnn.cpp**:

```
#include "simple_cnn.h"
SimpleCNN::SimpleCNN() {
    // Convolutional Block 1
    add(fl::Conv2D(3, 32, 3, 3, 1, 1, 1, 1)); // inChannels=3,
outChannels=32
    add(fl::BatchNorm(32));                   // Batch
Normalization
    add(fl::ReLU());
    add(fl::MaxPool2D(2, 2, 2, 2));
    add(fl::Dropout(0.25));                   // Dropout with
25% probability
    // Convolutional Block 2
    add(fl::Conv2D(32, 64, 3, 3, 1, 1, 1, 1));
    add(fl::BatchNorm(64));
    add(fl::ReLU());
    add(fl::MaxPool2D(2, 2, 2, 2));
    add(fl::Dropout(0.25));
    // Convolutional Block 3
    add(fl::Conv2D(64, 128, 3, 3, 1, 1, 1, 1));
```

```
    add(fl::BatchNorm(128));
    add(fl::ReLU());
    add(fl::MaxPool2D(2, 2, 2, 2));
    add(fl::Dropout(0.25));
    // Flatten the tensor
    add(fl::View({-1, 0, 0, 0}));
    // Fully Connected Layers
    add(fl::Linear(128 * 4 * 4, 256));
    add(fl::ReLU());
    add(fl::Dropout(0.5));
    add(fl::Linear(256, 10)); // CIFAR-10 classes
    add(fl::LogSoftmax());
}
```

In the above modifications, we've added Batch Normalization after each convolutional layer using **fl::BatchNorm**(numFeatures). And we also normalized the output of the convolutional layer before applying ReLU.

We also added dropout layers after the pooling layers and the fully connected layers. We used **fl::Dropout(p)**, where p is the dropout probability. Now here, it's pretty standard to use a dropout rate of 0.25 for convolutional layers and 0.5 for fully connected layers.

Adjust Training Code

In **main.cpp**, we set the model to training or evaluation mode appropriately.

```
// During training
model.train(); // Enables dropout and BatchNorm updates
// During validation/testing
model.eval(); // Disables dropout and uses running averages
for BatchNorm
```

From here onwards, no changes to the training loop are necessary beyond this point.

Following is the sample output:

```
Epoch [1/20], Train Loss: 1.750, Train Acc: 38.5%, Val Loss:
1.500, Val Acc: 45.0%
Epoch [2/20], Train Loss: 1.400, Train Acc: 50.0%, Val Loss:
1.300, Val Acc: 55.0%
...
Epoch [20/20], Train Loss: 0.500, Train Acc: 82.0%, Val Loss:
0.700, Val Acc: 75.0%
```

Now here, the gap between training and validation loss should be smaller compared to the model without dropout and batch normalization. You may also increase or decrease **p** in **fl::Dropout(p)** to see the effect on overfitting. If the model underfits (training accuracy is low), consider reducing the dropout rate.

To sum up, batch normalization stabilizes the learning process by normalizing layer inputs, allowing for higher learning rates and faster convergence. These techniques are widely adopted in deep learning and are essential tools in building effective neural networks.

Advanced Data Augmentation Strategies

Data augmentation is a powerful technique to artificially expand your dataset by applying transformations to the existing data. This helps prevent overfitting and improves the model's ability to generalize. It helps in following ways:

- Introducing variations that the model might encounter in real-world scenarios.
- By exposing the model to a wider range of data, it learns more generalized features.
- The model becomes more resilient to variations in input data.

Advanced Augmentation Techniques

Color Jittering

Color jittering is a pretty common data augmentation technique in machine learning, particularly in computer vision tasks. It basically means making random changes to the brightness, contrast, saturation, and hue of an image to simulate different lighting conditions and camera settings. Adding these variations helps the model work better in the real world, where images might look different because of things like lighting.

You can control how color jittering is implemented using the following several parameters.

- The brightness parameter controls how much the image brightness is adjusted, ranging from darker to lighter appearances.

- The contrast parameter changes the intensity difference between light and dark areas, which makes the image look sharper or softer.
- The saturation parameter affects the intensity of the colors, making them more vivid or muted.
- Finally, the hue parameter shifts the overall color tone of the image, introducing subtle or pronounced variations to the color palette.

These adjustments are made randomly within defined ranges, ensuring that the augmented dataset presents diverse examples for the model to learn from.

Random Erasing

This method is all about picking a random rectangular area in an image and erasing its pixels by swapping them out for random values or a constant. By simulating things like occlusions or missing parts in images, random erasing helps the model learn to focus on what's most important about an object, even when parts of it are hidden or missing.

Following are a few key things to keep in mind when You are implementing random erasing.

- The probability parameter determines how likely it is for the random erasing operation to be applied to a given image. This makes sure there's enough variety while keeping the original and augmented data in balance.
- The area range says how much of the image can be erased, so you can control the size of the occluded region.
- The aspect ratio range says what shapes the erased region can be, from narrow strips to more square-like areas.

These parameters work together to create different augmentations, which helps the model understand real-world scenarios where objects may not always be fully visible.

Implement Advanced Augmentations

Now here, we will enhance our **CIFAR10Dataset** class to include these advanced augmentations.

To begin with, first add any necessary includes:

```
#include <random>
#include <chrono>
```

Then, add augmentation functions within the class, such as:

- Color Jittering Function

```
fl::Tensor CIFAR10Dataset::colorJitter(fl::Tensor& image) {
    // Random generators
    static std::mt19937
gen(std::chrono::system_clock::now().time_since_epoch().count(
));
    // Define ranges for jittering
    std::uniform_real_distribution<float> brightnessDist(0.8f,
1.2f);
    std::uniform_real_distribution<float> contrastDist(0.8f,
1.2f);
    std::uniform_real_distribution<float> saturationDist(0.8f,
1.2f);
    std::uniform_real_distribution<float> hueDist(-0.1f,
0.1f);
    // Apply brightness adjustment
    float brightnessFactor = brightnessDist(gen);
    image = image * brightnessFactor;
    // Convert to HSV for saturation and hue adjustments
    // Note: Flashlight may not have built-in HSV conversion;
you might need to implement it or approximate it.
    // Apply contrast adjustment
    float contrastFactor = contrastDist(gen);
    image = ((image - 0.5f) * contrastFactor) + 0.5f;
    // Clamp the values to [0, 1]
    image = fl::clip(image, 0.0f, 1.0f);
    return image;
}
```

- Random Erasing Function

```
fl::Tensor CIFAR10Dataset::randomErasing(fl::Tensor& image) {
```

```
    static std::mt19937
gen(std::chrono::system_clock::now().time_since_epoch().count(
));
    float probability = 0.5f;
    std::uniform_real_distribution<float> probDist(0.0f,
1.0f);
    if (probDist(gen) > probability) {
        return image; // Do not apply erasing
    }
    // Parameters for erasing
    float sl = 0.02f; // Minimum proportion of erased area
    float sh = 0.4f;  // Maximum proportion of erased area
    float r1 = 0.3f;  // Minimum aspect ratio
    int imgH = image.dim(1);
    int imgW = image.dim(2);
    std::uniform_real_distribution<float> areaDist(sl, sh);
    std::uniform_real_distribution<float> aspectDist(r1, 1 /
r1);
    float targetArea = areaDist(gen) * imgH * imgW;
    float aspectRatio = aspectDist(gen);
    int h = static_cast<int>(std::round(std::sqrt(targetArea *
aspectRatio)));
    int w = static_cast<int>(std::round(std::sqrt(targetArea /
aspectRatio)));
    if (h < imgH && w < imgW) {
        std::uniform_int_distribution<int> heightDist(0, imgH
- h);
        std::uniform_int_distribution<int> widthDist(0, imgW -
w);
        int y = heightDist(gen);
        int x = widthDist(gen);
```

```
        // Erase the region
        std::uniform_real_distribution<float> eraseDist(0.0f,
1.0f);
        fl::Tensor eraseRegion = fl::full({image.dim(0), h,
w}, eraseDist(gen));
        // Replace the region in the image
        image(fl::span, fl::range(y, y + h - 1), fl::range(x,
x + w - 1)) = eraseRegion;
    }
    return image;
}
```

Now here do make a note that the functions handle the data types and dimensions correctly. The code may require adjustments based on the actual API of the Flashlight library.

Next after updating the dataset, retrain the model to observe the impact.

```
// In main.cpp, the training code remains largely the same
// Initialize the dataset with augmentations
CIFAR10Dataset trainDataset(trainData, true);
```

Here, the model should perform better on validation and test sets due to exposure to more diverse data.

Following is the sample training output:

```
Epoch [1/20], Train Loss: 1.800, Train Acc: 36.0%, Val Loss:
1.500, Val Acc: 46.0%
Epoch [2/20], Train Loss: 1.450, Train Acc: 48.0%, Val Loss:
1.300, Val Acc: 56.0%
...
Epoch [20/20], Train Loss: 0.550, Train Acc: 80.0%, Val Loss:
0.650, Val Acc: 78.0%
```

In the above output, if you see an improvement in validation accuracy, then it indicates better generalization. The gap between training and validation accuracy may decrease overall.

Hyperparameter Tuning

Hyperparameter Overview

Hyperparameter tuning is a really important part of getting a neural network to work as well as it can. Hyperparameters are the settings that control how the training is done and the way the model is set up, like learning rates, batch sizes, number of layers and number of neurons. Unlike model parameters, hyperparameters aren't learned during training and have to be set before the training starts.

Following are some of the very common hyperparameters to tune:

1. Learning Rate
2. Batch Size
3. Optimizer Type
4. Number of Epochs
5. Model Architecture Parameters
    - Number of layers
    - Number of neurons/filters
    - Activation functions

Approaches to Hyperparameter Tuning

There are several approaches to tuning hyperparameters, each with its strengths and limitations.

- **`Manual search`** is the simplest approach, where one adjusts a single hyperparameter at a time based on intuition or prior experience. While it is straightforward and requires minimal setup, this method often fails to identify the optimal combination of hyperparameters, especially for complex models or large parameter spaces.
- **`Grid search`** takes a systematic approach by defining a grid of possible values for each hyperparameter and then training and evaluating the model for every possible combination. Although grid search is exhaustive and ensures that no combination is overlooked, it is computationally expensive, particularly when the hyperparameter space has many dimensions or large ranges.
- **`Random search`** offers a more efficient alternative to grid search by randomly sampling hyperparameters from predefined distributions rather than exhaustively trying all combinations. This approach is especially effective in high-dimensional spaces, as it often uncovers good hyperparameter combinations with fewer evaluations compared to grid search.

- **Bayesian optimization** represents a more sophisticated method, using probabilistic models to select hyperparameters based on the results of previous evaluations. This iterative approach is highly efficient, focusing computational resources on promising regions of the hyperparameter space. However, it is more complex to implement and may require additional tools or libraries.

Implementing Hyperparameter Tuning

We will focus on manual and random search methods due to their simplicity.

Tuning Learning Rate

How does the learning rate affect the outcome? If it's too high, it can have some pretty negative effects. This can cause the loss to fluctuate or even diverge. And if it's too low, it'll take longer to train and it'll converge more slowly.

Here's something to try the experiment with learning rates. We can test the learning rates like 0.1, 0.01, 0.001, 0.0001 and then observe what happens to our training and validation loss as below:

```
std::vector<float> learningRates = {0.1f, 0.01f, 0.001f,
0.0001f};
for (float lr : learningRates) {
    // Initialize model, optimizer, and other components
    SimpleCNN model;
    auto criterion = fl::NegativeLogLikelihood();
    fl::AdamOptimizer optimizer(model.params(), lr);

    // Training loop
    // ...

    // Record performance metrics
    // ...
}
```

After this, let's take a look at the results. For this, we first plot the training and validation loss curves for each learning rate. Then, we will choose the learning rate that strikes the best balance between convergence speed and stability.

Tuning Batch Size

When it comes to small batch sizes, there are a few things to keep in mind. First, it provides noisy gradient estimates. On the plus side, they can generalize better, but it can also slow down training.

With regards to large batch sizes, it offers more stable gradients and they require more memory and may lead to poor generalization.

Let's experiment with batch sizes. Here, try testing batch sizes in the ranges of 32, 64, 128, and 256. Try adjusting the learning rates if you need to. With larger batch sizes, you can often get away with a higher learning rate.

```
std::vector<int> batchSizes = {32, 64, 128, 256};
for (int bs : batchSizes) {
    // Adjust data loaders
    auto trainBatchDataset = fl::BatchDataset(
        std::make_shared<CIFAR10Dataset>(trainDataset),
        bs
    );
    auto trainDataLoader =
fl::PrefetchDataset(trainBatchDataset, 4);

    // Initialize model, optimizer, and other components
    SimpleCNN model;
    auto criterion = fl::NegativeLogLikelihood();
    fl::AdamOptimizer optimizer(model.params(), learningRate);

    // Training loop
    // ...

    // Record performance metrics
    // ...
}
```

For results,

- Keep an eye on how long the training takes per epoch.
- Keep an eye on how this affects the model's accuracy and loss.
- Pick a batch size that strikes a good balance between training speed and performance.

By systematically experimenting with different settings and carefully analyzing the results, you can find the optimal configuration for your specific problem. Remember that hyperparameters often interact in complex ways, so iterative testing and refinement are essential.

Summary

Overall, we worked on improving our neural network models to get better results and make them more versatile. We started by looking at why overfitting happens and how it can stop a model from working well with new data. To beat overfitting, we looked at different techniques like regularization methods, simplifying the model architecture, and implementing early stopping based on validation performance.

Next, we looked at some practical strategies, like incorporating dropout and batch normalization into our models. I also found out that dropout helps prevent over-reliance on specific neurons by randomly dropping them during training. We also looked into more complex data manipulation techniques, like color jittering and random erasing. These help create more variety in our data set, which makes the models more reliable. We also focused on tuning the settings for the models. We tweaked things like the learning rates and batch sizes, among other parameters. We also learned to analyze and interpret the results. We used confusion matrices and classification reports, which give us a deeper understanding of how the models are performing and help us identify where we can make improvements.

CHAPTER 7: ADVANCED NEURAL NETWORK ARCHITECTURES

Chapter Overview

In this chapter, we will take a look at some of the most cutting-edge neural network architectures that have really taken the field of deep learning to the next level. We will start with ResNet and look at how these architectures have tackled issues like the vanishing gradient problem, making it possible to train extremely deep networks. We will put together a ResNet-like model using the Flashlight, so we can get some hands-on experience with modern architectures.

Next, we will look at transfer learning, which is a great technique that uses pre-trained models to solve new but related tasks, saving time and computational resources. We will learn about how to use transfer learning in C++, adapting existing models to fit our needs. Finally, we will focus on making models more efficient, looking at ways to reduce the amount of work they do and improve performance without losing accuracy.

By the end of this chapter, You will have a good understanding of advanced architectures and the skills you need to implement and optimize them for your machine learning projects.

Exploring ResNet

The deeper neural networks got, the more complex patterns they had to capture. This led to some big challenges, like the vanishing gradient problem. This happens when gradients get really small during backpropagation, which makes it hard to train the first few layers in very deep networks. To fix this, people came up with new architectures like ResNet, which changed the game of deep learning by letting us train networks with hundreds or even thousands of layers.

Understanding ResNet (Residual Networks)

ResNet, introduced by Kaiming He et al. in 2015, proposed a novel architecture that made training very deep networks feasible. The key innovation was the introduction of **residual blocks**, which allow the network to learn residual functions with reference to the layer inputs.

Some of the key concepts:

- **Residual Learning:** Instead of each layer learning an underlying mapping $H(x)H(x)H(x)$, residual blocks let layers fit a residual mapping $F(x) = H(x) - xF(x) = H(x) - xF(x) = H(x) - x$, reformulating the original mapping as $H(x) = F(x) + xH(x) = F(x) + xH(x) = F(x) + x$.
- **Shortcut Connections:** Identity mappings that skip one or more layers, directly connecting the input of a residual block to its output.
- **Ease of Optimization:** Gradients can flow more easily backward through the network, mitigating the vanishing gradient problem.

Residual Block Structure

A basic residual block can be represented as:

$$\text{Output} = F(x, \{Wi\}) + x$$

Where:

- $F(x, \{Wi\})$ is the residual mapping to be learned.
- x is the input to the block.
- The addition is performed element-wise.

Building on the success of ResNet, researchers have developed various architectures to further enhance performance and efficiency, such as:

DenseNet (Dense Convolutional Network)

DenseNet, or Dense Convolutional Network, was introduced by Gao Huang and colleagues in 2017. It employs a distinctive architecture where each layer is directly connected to all preceding layers, promoting an efficient reuse of features throughout the network. This connectivity significantly enhances the flow of information and gradients, which helps mitigate the vanishing gradient problem that often occurs in deep neural networks. Additionally, this design allows DenseNet to use parameters more efficiently by reducing redundancy, leading to a model that is both powerful and lightweight compared to traditional convolutional architectures.

Inception Networks

Inception, introduced by Szegedy et al. from Google in 2014, incorporates an innovative architecture that uses parallel convolutional layers with varying kernel sizes within a single module, known as the Inception module. This design allows the network to effectively capture spatial correlations at multiple scales, enhancing its ability to process complex visual patterns. Over time, the architecture evolved through several iterations, from Inception-v1 to Inception-v4, with each version incorporating progressive improvements in module design. These advancements not only refined the model's accuracy and efficiency but also significantly reduced computational costs, making the architecture highly suitable for practical applications.

MobileNet

MobileNet, introduced by Howard et al. in 2017, was specifically designed to address the challenges of deploying deep learning models on mobile and embedded devices with limited computational resources. The architecture achieves this efficiency through innovative techniques such as depthwise separable convolutions, which decompose a standard convolution operation into two steps: a depthwise convolution that applies a single filter per input channel, followed by a pointwise convolution that combines these outputs. This factorization significantly reduces computational overhead while maintaining performance. Additionally, MobileNet incorporates width and resolution multipliers, which allow adjustments to the network's width and input resolution. These multipliers enable a flexible trade-off between latency and accuracy, making MobileNet highly adaptable to various resource constrained environments.

EfficientNet

EfficientNet, introduced by Tan and Le in 2019, presents a structured approach to scaling up deep learning models using a compound scaling method. This method systematically adjusts the network's depth, width, and input resolution in a balanced manner, optimizing model performance across these dimensions. By leveraging this strategy, EfficientNet achieves higher accuracy while using fewer parameters compared to traditional scaling methods. Its efficient design ensures an optimal trade-off between model complexity and performance, making it well-suited for a wide range of applications.

The ResNet architecture itself includes several variants such as ResNet-18, ResNet-34, ResNet-50, ResNet-101, and ResNet-152, which differ primarily in their depth, as indicated by the number in their names. The depth reflects the total number of layers in the network, with deeper architectures designed to capture more complex features. For deeper versions, starting from ResNet-50, bottleneck blocks are employed to optimize computational efficiency. These blocks reduce the number of parameters by compressing and expanding feature maps, enabling deeper networks to maintain performance without excessive computational overhead.

Next, We will look at putting together a ResNet-like model using Flashlight. This will let us try out these ideas in practice and make our model work even better.

Implementing a ResNet-like Model

Here, we will now implement a simplified version of ResNet using Flashlight's modular layers. Before we begin with, do consider the following is the basic residual block structure:

- Convolutional Layer
- Batch Normalization
- Activation Function (ReLU)
- Convolutional Layer
- Batch Normalization
- Skip Connection (Addition)
- Activation Function (ReLU)

Create and Implement Residual Block Class

We will start with defining a class **ResidualBlock** that inherits from **fl::Module**.

```
// residual_block.h
#ifndef RESIDUAL_BLOCK_H
#define RESIDUAL_BLOCK_H
#include <flashlight/flashlight.h>
class ResidualBlock : public fl::Module {
public:
    ResidualBlock(int inChannels, int outChannels, int stride
= 1, bool useProjection = false);
    fl::Variable forward(const fl::Variable& input) override;
private:
    std::shared_ptr<fl::Sequential> convBlock_;
    std::shared_ptr<fl::Sequential> shortcut_;
};
#endif // RESIDUAL_BLOCK_H
```

Next, we then implement the residual block:

```
// residual_block.cpp
#include "residual_block.h"
ResidualBlock::ResidualBlock(int inChannels, int outChannels,
int stride, bool useProjection) {
    convBlock_ = std::make_shared<fl::Sequential>();
    convBlock_->add(fl::Conv2D(inChannels, outChannels, 3, 3,
stride, stride, 1, 1));
    convBlock_->add(fl::BatchNorm(outChannels));
    convBlock_->add(fl::ReLU());
    convBlock_->add(fl::Conv2D(outChannels, outChannels, 3, 3,
1, 1, 1, 1));
    convBlock_->add(fl::BatchNorm(outChannels));
```

```
    if (useProjection || stride != 1 || inChannels !=
outChannels) {
        shortcut_ = std::make_shared<fl::Sequential>();
        shortcut_->add(fl::Conv2D(inChannels, outChannels, 1,
1, stride, stride));
        shortcut_->add(fl::BatchNorm(outChannels));
    } else {
        shortcut_ = nullptr; // Identity shortcut
    }
}
fl::Variable ResidualBlock::forward(const fl::Variable& input)
{
    auto residual = convBlock_->forward(input);
    fl::Variable shortcutOutput;
    if (shortcut_) {
        shortcutOutput = shortcut_->forward(input);
    } else {
        shortcutOutput = input;
    }
    auto output = fl::ReLU()(residual + shortcutOutput);
    return output;
}
```

Given below is a quick breakdown of the code above:

- **convBlock_** is the main path, made up of two convolutional layers with BatchNorm and ReLU.
- **shortcut_** is used to adjust the input dimensions if needed, using a 1x1 convolution and BatchNorm.
- And, **forward Function** is where the residual is computed, added to the shortcut connection, and ReLU activation is applied.

Building ResNet-like Model

Now, we move on to constructing a simplified ResNet model by stacking multiple residual blocks. For this, we create a new model class:

```
// resnet_model.h
#ifndef RESNET_MODEL_H
#define RESNET_MODEL_H
#include <flashlight/flashlight.h>
#include "residual_block.h"
class ResNetModel : public fl::Module {
public:
    ResNetModel(int numClasses = 10);
    fl::Variable forward(const fl::Variable& input) override;
private:
    std::shared_ptr<fl::Sequential> layers_;
};
#endif // RESNET_MODEL_H
```

Next, we implement the ResNet model:

```
// resnet_model.cpp
#include "resnet_model.h"
ResNetModel::ResNetModel(int numClasses) {
    layers_ = std::make_shared<fl::Sequential>();
    // Initial convolution and pooling
    layers_->add(fl::Conv2D(3, 64, 7, 7, 2, 2, 3, 3));
    layers_->add(fl::BatchNorm(64));
    layers_->add(fl::ReLU());
    layers_->add(fl::MaxPool2D(3, 3, 2, 2, 1, 1));
    // Define the layers with residual blocks
    // For simplicity, we will implement a ResNet-18-like
structure
    int inChannels = 64;
```

```
    std::vector<int> layersConfig = {2, 2, 2, 2}; // Number of
blocks in each layer
    std::vector<int> outChannelsList = {64, 128, 256, 512};
    for (size_t i = 0; i < layersConfig.size(); ++i) {
        int outChannels = outChannelsList[i];
        int numBlocks = layersConfig[i];
        int stride = (i == 0) ? 1 : 2; // Downsample at the
beginning of each layer except the first
        // First block in the layer
        layers_-
>add(std::make_shared<ResidualBlock>(inChannels, outChannels,
stride, (stride != 1 || inChannels != outChannels)));
        // Remaining blocks
        for (int j = 1; j < numBlocks; ++j) {
            layers_-
>add(std::make_shared<ResidualBlock>(outChannels,
outChannels));
        }
        inChannels = outChannels;
    }
    // Global average pooling and fully connected layer
    layers_->add(fl::AdaptiveAvgPool2D(1, 1));
    layers_->add(fl::View({-1}));
    layers_->add(fl::Linear(512, numClasses));
    layers_->add(fl::LogSoftmax());
}
fl::Variable ResNetModel::forward(const fl::Variable& input) {
    return layers_->forward(input);
}
```

In **main.cpp**, we will replace the previous model with our new **ResNetModel**.

```
#include "resnet_model.h"
// Initialize the ResNet model
ResNetModel model(numClasses);
// Define loss function and optimizer
auto criterion = fl::NegativeLogLikelihood();
float learningRate = 0.1; // ResNets often start with a higher
learning rate
fl::SGDOptimizer optimizer(model.params(), learningRate, 0.9);
// Using SGD with Momentum
```

Adjust Learning Rate Scheduler

ResNets often use learning rate scheduling to improve training. We can configure the rate scheduler as shown below:

```
int epochDecay = 30;
float decayRate = 0.1;
for (int epoch = 1; epoch <= numEpochs; ++epoch) {
    // Adjust learning rate
    if (epoch % epochDecay == 0) {
        learningRate *= decayRate;
        optimizer.setLr(learningRate);
    }
    // Training and validation loops
    // ...
}
```

You may need to adjust **numEpochs**, batch sizes, and other hyperparameters if the computational resources are not getting suited to our model.

After this, before compiling and running the program, get all source files are included in your **CMakeLists.txt**.

```
add_executable(ml_project
    src/main.cpp
```

```
    src/cifar10_loader.cpp
    src/cifar10_dataset.cpp
    src/residual_block.cpp
    src/resnet_model.cpp
)
```

Now, finally we compile and run the program:

```
cd ~/ml_project/build
cmake ..
make
./ml_project
```

Following is the expected and possible output:

```
Epoch [1/90], Train Loss: 1.900, Train Acc: 30.0%, Val Loss: 1.700, Val Acc: 40.0%
Epoch [2/90], Train Loss: 1.600, Train Acc: 42.0%, Val Loss: 1.500, Val Acc: 45.0%
...
Epoch [90/90], Train Loss: 0.200, Train Acc: 95.0%, Val Loss: 0.500, Val Acc: 85.0%
```

Let's take a look at the results, wherein we will see:

- how the training and validation loss change over epochs.
- keep an eye on overfitting and think about stopping early if we need to.
- compare the ResNet model's accuracy with previous models.
- how much better the validation and test accuracy are.

By putting a ResNet-like model together, we've got some hands-on experience with the ins and outs of advanced neural network architectures and it also gives you the tools to try out and adapt the latest models for your own projects.

Understanding Transfer Learning

Why Transfer Learning and How it Works?

Transfer learning is a machine learning technique where a model developed for one task is repurposed as the starting point for a model on a second, related task. Instead of training a model from scratch, this approach leverages the knowledge learned by a pre-trained model on a large dataset and adapts it to a new task. Key concepts in transfer learning include the use of pre-trained models—such as those trained on extensive datasets like ImageNet—as a foundation. Feature extraction is a crucial step, where the learned features from the pre-trained model are used as inputs to a new model. Fine-tuning involves slightly adjusting the weights of the pre-trained model to better fit the specifics of the new task.

Transfer learning offers several significant advantages. Firstly, it reduces training time; training deep networks from scratch demands substantial time and computational resources, whereas transfer learning allows for faster convergence by building upon existing models. Secondly, it can lead to improved performance. Pre-trained models have already learned rich feature representations that can enhance performance on related tasks, which is particularly beneficial when the new dataset is small. Lastly, transfer learning helps overcome data limitations. In scenarios with limited labeled data, it enables effective model training by utilizing knowledge from larger, related datasets.

The process of transfer learning typically involves two main strategies: feature extraction and fine-tuning. In feature extraction, the early layers of a neural network—which capture general features like edges and textures—are kept unchanged to retain their learned representations. The final layers, responsible for task-specific outputs, are replaced with new layers suitable for the new task and are trained from scratch. Fine-tuning takes this a step further by unfreezing some of the pre-trained layers after training the new layers. The entire network or selected layers are then trained with a low learning rate to fine-tune the weights, allowing the model to adjust more precisely to the new task. Often, a combination of both approaches is used: starting with feature extraction and then proceeding to fine-tuning for further improvements.

Applications and Benefits

Transfer learning is widely applied across various domains. In image classification, models trained on ImageNet are adapted to classify different sets of images, benefiting from the extensive visual features already learned. In object detection and segmentation, pre-trained backbones are used in models like Faster R-CNN or Mask R-CNN to identify and segment objects within images. In natural language processing, models such as BERT or GPT are utilized for tasks like language translation, sentiment analysis, and text generation. In speech recognition, models trained on large speech datasets are applied to specific language domains, improving accuracy and reducing training time.

The efficiency of transfer learning lies in its ability to save time and resources by reusing existing models. This not only accelerates the development process but also reduces the computational power required. The performance boost is another significant benefit; leveraging learned features often leads to better results than training from scratch, especially when data is limited. Additionally, transfer learning offers flexibility, as it can be applied across different domains and tasks, making it a versatile tool in the machine learning toolkit.

Despite its advantages, transfer learning comes with challenges. Domain similarity is crucial; transfer learning is most effective when the source and target tasks are related. If the tasks are too dissimilar, the pre-trained features may not be applicable, leading to poor performance. Overfitting is another concern; fine-tuning with a small dataset can cause the model to overfit to the training data, necessitating the use of regularization techniques or data augmentation. Licensing and usage rights must also be considered to ensure that pre-trained models are used in compliance with their licenses, especially in commercial applications.

Transfer Learning Use-case

There are several strategies for implementing transfer learning. In full network transfer, the entire pre-trained model is used without modifications, which is suitable for tasks very similar to the original task. Partial network transfer involves using only certain layers or parts of the pre-trained model, adjusting based on the relevance of features to the new task. Parameter transfer initializes the new model with parameters from the pre-trained model, and all layers are retrained but start from a pre-trained state, providing a head start over random initialization.

For example, consider the task of classifying medical images into different disease categories. The approach would begin by selecting a pre-trained model, such as ResNet or VGG, trained on ImageNet. The model is then modified by replacing the final classification layer with a new layer that matches the number of disease categories. During the feature extraction phase, the convolutional base is frozen to retain general features learned from the large dataset. In the fine-tuning phase, some of the top layers are unfrozen to adjust the model to the specific features of medical images. Training involves using a smaller learning rate for fine-tuning and applying data augmentation techniques to mitigate overfitting due to the typically small size of medical image datasets.

In transfer learning, by utilizing pre-trained models, you can achieve high performance with less data and reduced training time.

Transfer Learning in Action

Now we will take the concepts of transfer learning previously discussed and apply them practically. We will demonstrate how to load a pre-trained model and fine-tune it on a new dataset. This approach can significantly reduce training time and improve performance, especially when dealing with limited data.

Here, we alreadt have a function or method to load a pre-trained ResNet-18 model:

```
#include <flashlight/flashlight.h>
```

```
// Function to load a pre-trained ResNet-18 model
std::shared_ptr<fl::Module> loadPretrainedResNet18();
```

Since Flashlight may not provide pre-trained models directly, you might need to load the model weights from a file or convert them from another framework like PyTorch. So here, we will proceed as if we have a function **loadPretrainedResNet18()** that returns a pre-trained model.

Modify Final Layers

The pre-trained ResNet-18 model is trained to classify images into 1000 classes (ImageNet). We need to modify the final layer to output 10 classes for CIFAR-10.

So here, we wiil extract the convolutional base:

```
auto pretrainedModel = loadPretrainedResNet18();
// Remove the final classification layer
pretrainedModel->modules().pop_back(); // Remove LogSoftmax
pretrainedModel->modules().pop_back(); // Remove Linear layer
```

Next, we then add new classification layers:

```
// Add new layers for CIFAR-10
pretrainedModel->add(fl::Linear(512, 10)); // 512 is the
output size before the final layer
pretrainedModel->add(fl::LogSoftmax());
```

Since CIFAR-10 images are 32x32 pixels, and the original ResNet expects 224x224 images, we need to resize the images.

```
// In your data loading code, resize images to 224x224
image = fl::resize(image, 224, 224);
```

Alternatively, we can adjust the model to work with smaller images by changing the stride and kernel size of the initial convolutional layer.

```
// Modify the first convolutional layer
auto conv1 =
std::dynamic_pointer_cast<fl::Conv2D>(pretrainedModel-
>modules()[0]);
```

```
conv1->setParams(fl::Conv2D(3, 64, 3, 3, 1, 1, 1, 1)-
>params());
```

Now, in order to use the pre-trained weights effectively, we can freeze some or all of the pre-trained layers during initial training.

```
for (auto& module : pretrainedModel->modules()) {
    module->train(false); // Set module to evaluation mode
    for (auto& param : module->params()) {
        param.setGrad(false); // Disable gradient computation
    }
}
// Unfreeze the new classification layers
auto classifier = pretrainedModel->modules().back();
classifier->train(true);
for (auto& param : classifier->params()) {
    param.setGrad(true);
}
```

We then define loss function and optimizer:

```
auto criterion = fl::NegativeLogLikelihood();
float learningRate = 0.001;
fl::AdamOptimizer optimizer(pretrainedModel->params(),
learningRate);
```

Here, the training loop remains similar to previous implementations as below.

```
for (int epoch = 1; epoch <= numEpochs; ++epoch) {
    // Training phase
    pretrainedModel->train(); // Set model to training mode
    float trainLoss = 0.0;
    int correctTrain = 0;
    int totalTrain = 0;
```

```
    for (auto& batch : *trainDataLoader) {
        auto inputs = batch[0];
        auto targets = batch[1];
        // Move data to GPU if available
        if (fl::cuda::isAvailable()) {
            inputs = inputs.to(fl::dtype::f32,
fl::MemoryLocation::CUDA);
            targets = targets.to(fl::dtype::s32,
fl::MemoryLocation::CUDA);
        }
        fl::Variable inputVar(inputs, false);
        fl::Variable targetVar(targets, false);
        // Forward pass
        auto outputs = pretrainedModel->forward(inputVar);
        // Compute loss
        auto loss = criterion(outputs, targetVar);
        // Backward pass and optimization
        optimizer.zeroGrad();
        loss.backward();
        optimizer.step();
        // Accumulate training loss and accuracy
        trainLoss += loss.scalar<float>();
        auto predictions = fl::argmax(outputs.tensor(), 0);
        auto targetTensor =
targetVar.tensor().astype(fl::dtype::s32);
        correctTrain += fl::count(predictions ==
targetTensor).asScalar<int>();
        totalTrain += batchSize;
    }
    // Validation and logging code
```

```
    // ...
}
```

After training the new layers, we can unfreeze some of the pre-trained layers and fine-tune the model with a lower learning rate.

```
// Unfreeze the top few layers
for (size_t i = pretrainedModel->modules().size() - 5; i < pretrainedModel->modules().size(); ++i) {
    auto module = pretrainedModel->modules()[i];
    module->train(true);
    for (auto& param : module->params()) {
        param.setGrad(true);
    }
}
// Adjust learning rate for fine-tuning
float fineTuneLearningRate = 1e-4;
optimizer.setLr(fineTuneLearningRate);
```

In case needed, we can move on to additional epochs in order to fine-tune the model.

Handle Pre-trained Model Loading

If Flashlight doesn't support loading pre-trained models directly, we can also convert models from other frameworks. We can convert models from frameworks like PyTorch or TensorFlow to ONNX (Open Neural Network Exchange) format.

To do this, we simply load the ONNX model into Flashlight as shown below:

```
#include <flashlight/fl/tensor/Index.h>
#include <flashlight/fl/nn/modules/Container.h>
#include <flashlight/fl/optim/Optimizers.h>
#include <flashlight/fl/contrib/modules/Onnx.h>
// Load the ONNX model
```

```
std::shared_ptr<fl::Module> pretrainedModel =
fl::loadOnnx("resnet18.onnx");
```

Now here, we need to ensure that the necessary dependencies and configurations are in place for ONNX support as well otherwise it may not work properly. Also, since the pre-trained model expects a specific input size, you may need to adjust the images or the model.

For example, resize CIFAR-10 images to the expected input size (e.g., 224x224).

```
image = fl::resize(image, 224, 224);
```

We can also adjust the initial layers to accept smaller images.

By applying transfer learning in C++, we've demonstrated how to leverage pre-trained models to improve training efficiency and performance. This approach is particularly valuable when working with limited data or computational resources.

Optimizing Model Efficiency

Inevitably, as neural networks get bigger and more complex, they start to use more and more resources. In order to make them more efficient, we need to make them smaller and less computationally demanding without losing any accuracy. This is especially important for deploying models in environments where resources are limited, such as mobile devices or real-time systems.

We have listed some of the techniques for model optimization as below:

1. Model Pruning
2. Quantization
3. Knowledge Distillation
4. Efficient Network Architectures
5. Hardware-Specific Optimizations

Model Pruning

Model pruning involves removing unnecessary weights or neurons from a neural network. By identifying and eliminating redundant parameters, we can reduce the model size and computation.

Following are some of the types of pruning:

- The first is **`weight pruning`**, which involves setting individual weights to zero based on a threshold. This method identifies less important weights and effectively eliminates them, creating a sparse representation of the network.

- The second is **`neuron pruning`**, where entire neurons or filters are removed. This type of pruning focuses on larger structural components of the model, such as filters in convolutional layers or neurons in fully connected layers, to simplify the architecture.

The process of pruning usually starts with a fully trained model. The first step is to take a look at the model's parameters—weights or neurons—and see which are the most important. If a parameter falls below a certain level, we consider it to be redundant. In the case of weights, we set it to zero. For neurons, we remove them entirely. The model is then fine-tuned by retraining it on the dataset to make up for any loss in accuracy caused by the pruning process. The fine-tuning step makes sure that the network performs as well as possible with the reduced complexity.

Here, you need to make a note that pruning introduces a trade-off between sparsity and accuracy. If you prune too much, it can really hurt the model's performance, making it less effective for the task at hand. On top of that, sparse models are smaller in terms of computing power, but they might not be any faster unless the hardware can handle optimized operations for sparse matrices. So, it's important to find the right balance between pruning and maintaining the desired level of accuracy.

Quantization

This quantization is a technique used in machine learning to make models more efficient by reducing the precision of the numbers used to represent model parameters. Instead of using high-precision formats like 32-bit floating-point, quantization uses lower-precision formats like 8-bit integers. This reduction in precision has a big impact on how efficiently machine learning models can be run, especially in environments where memory and computational resources are limited.

The main benefit of quantization is that it makes models smaller because lower-precision numbers take up less memory. This makes them easier to use on devices with limited storage or memory, like mobile phones or embedded systems. Another advantage is that it can make predictions faster because lower-precision data can be processed more quickly. This is great for apps that need to make predictions in real time or for apps that are used on edge devices.

Now here, there are two main approaches to quantization:

- Post-training quantization involves quantizing a trained model directly without any additional training. This method is simple and quick to implement but may lead to some accuracy loss.
- Quantization-aware training, on the other hand, incorporates the effects of quantization during the training process. By simulating lower-precision computations during training, this approach helps maintain accuracy, ensuring the model performs well even after being quantized.

Now in our Flashlight setup, quantization can be achieved using utilities or by configuring the model to use lower-precision data types as shown below:

```
// Configure to use 16-bit floating-point precision
fl::dtype dataType = fl::dtype::f16;
```

Now it also equally important to make a note that the quantization can introduce accuracy loss, as reducing precision may result in small errors in calculations. This can be mitigated by using quantization-aware training, which helps the model adapt to lower precision during training. Another important consideration is hardware support. Not all devices support lower-precision computations natively, so it is also needed to verify that the deployment environment is compatible with quantized models to realize the benefits of reduced computation and memory requirements.

Knowledge Distillation

This knowledge distillation is another machine learning technique where a smaller model, known as the student, is trained to replicate the behavior of a larger, high-performing model, referred to as the teacher. This process enables the smaller model to inherit the capabilities of the larger one while being more efficient in terms of size and computational requirements. The essence of knowledge distillation lies in transferring the knowledge encoded in the teacher's predictions to the student model. Here, the process begins by training the teacher model, typically a large neural network with high accuracy. Once the teacher model is trained, its outputs, often referred to as soft labels, are used as targets to guide the training of the student model. These soft labels contain rich information about the relationships between classes, which helps the student model approximate the teacher's predictions more effectively than training solely on true labels.

The implementation of knowledge distillation involves several steps.

- First, a student model with a smaller network architecture is defined to serve as the lightweight alternative to the teacher.
- Next, a loss function is designed to combine the standard loss—such as cross-entropy with the true labels—and a distillation loss that measures the divergence between the teacher's outputs and the student's predictions, often using metrics like Kullback-Leibler (KL) divergence.

During the training loop, the teacher's outputs are computed for a given input. These outputs are then compared with the student's predictions to calculate the distillation loss. The combined loss is used to update the parameters of the student model, enabling it to learn from both the true labels and the teacher's guidance.

Let us look below for a quick example of implementation:

```
// Compute teacher outputs (without gradient computation)
auto teacherOutputs = teacherModel-
>forward(inputVar).tensor().copy();
```

```
teacherOutputs.setGrad(false);
// Compute student outputs
auto studentOutputs = studentModel->forward(inputVar);
// Calculate distillation loss
auto distillationLoss = fl::mean(fl::klDiv(studentOutputs,
teacherOutputs));
// Combine with standard loss
auto standardLoss = criterion(studentOutputs, targetVar);
auto totalLoss = alpha * standardLoss + (1 - alpha) *
distillationLoss;
```

Here, the parameter **alpha** controls the trade-off between standard loss and distillation loss.

Efficient Network Architectures

Efficient network architectures are designed to strike a balance between performance and computational efficiency. They're faster and lighter without significantly compromising accuracy. Some examples of these architectures are MobileNet, ShuffleNet, and SqueezeNet. Each one uses new and creative ways to make networks more efficient.

One of the main techniques used in efficient architectures is depthwise separable convolutions, which separate spatial and channel-wise operations in convolutional layers. This cuts down on the number of computations and parameters a lot more than standard convolutions do. Another common approach is group convolutions, where channels are split into smaller groups, allowing for parallel computations with fewer parameters. Fire modules, which were introduced in SqueezeNet, use 1x1 convolutions to reduce channel dimensions, followed by a mix of 1x1 and 3x3 convolutions to balance computation and representational capacity.

Let us now try implementing efficient layers:

```
// Depthwise convolution layer
auto depthwiseConv = std::make_shared<fl::Conv2D>(
    inChannels, inChannels, kernelSize, kernelSize, stride,
stride, padding, padding, inChannels);
```

Similarly, a pointwise convolution layer, often used in conjunction with depthwise convolutions to adjust the number of output channels, is implemented with a 1x1 kernel:

```
// Pointwise convolution layer
```

```
auto pointwiseConv = std::make_shared<fl::Conv2D>(
    inChannels, outChannels, 1, 1, 1, 1, 0, 0);
```

The other efficient architectures like MobileNet often stack these efficient layers into reusable blocks. A typical MobileNet block combines depthwise and pointwise convolutions, with batch normalization and activation functions applied after each operation:

```
// MobileNet block implementation
add(depthwiseConv);
add(fl::BatchNorm(inChannels));
add(fl::ReLU());
add(pointwiseConv);
add(fl::BatchNorm(outChannels));
add(fl::ReLU());
```

This modular design ensures both computational efficiency and ease of extension, enabling developers to customize the network as needed.

Regarding the efficient architectures, these are frequently optimized for specific hardware features, such as GPUs or specialized accelerators, to maximize their performance gains. So there has to be a close eye at consideration of the target deployment environment.

Summary

To wrap up this chapter, we looked at some of the most advanced neural network architectures, with a focus on how ResNets have transformed deep learning. We looked at how ResNet tackled the vanishing gradient problem through residual learning, which lets you train ultra-deep networks with better accuracy and generalization. By putting together, a simplified version of a ResNet-like model using Flashlight, we got some hands-on experience in building and training these complex systems. It helped us improve how well our model performs on these challenging tasks.

We also learned about transfer learning, which uses pre-trained models to make training more efficient and improve performance, especially when there isn't a lot of data. We also showed how to use transfer learning to load and fine-tune a pre-trained model in Flashlight, which cuts down on training time and computing resources. Finally, we looked at ways to make models more efficient, like pruning, quantization, and knowledge distillation, to reduce the model size and computing requirements without losing accuracy.

CHAPTER 8: DEPLOYMENT AND INTEGRATION

Chapter Overview

This is a very short chapter and in this chapter, we will move from developing models to deploying and integrating our neural networks into real applications. We will start by learning how to save and load models, ensuring that our trained networks can be serialized and reused efficiently. Next, we will explore integrating the model into applications, discussing how to embed our neural networks into software systems, APIs, or services. And then finally, we will focus on real-time inference, assessing techniques to enable our models to make predictions quickly and efficiently in live environments.

Saving and Loading Models

When working with neural networks, it's essential to be able to save trained models for future use, whether for inference, further training, or sharing with others. Serialization allows us to store the model's architecture and learned parameters to disk and load them later without retraining. In this section, we will learn how to save and load models using the Flashlight library, ensuring that our efforts in training can be effectively utilized in deployment.

Saving Models

The Flashlight tool lets you save the state of models, optimizers, and other training components. The main way to do this is by serializing the model's parameters and any necessary metadata.

Saving Model Parameters

To save the model's parameters, we can use the **fl::save** function, which serializes the model to a file.

For example:

```
#include <flashlight/flashlight.h>
// After training the model
std::string modelPath = "trained_model.bin";
fl::save(modelPath, model);
```

Here are the details:

- **modelPath** is where you want to save the file with the model.
- And, **fl::save** will save all the model's parameters to that file.

Saving Additional Training State

If you want to save the optimizer state or other training information (e.g., epoch number), you can serialize them as well.

For example:

```
std::string optimizerPath = "optimizer_state.bin";
fl::save(optimizerPath, optimizer);
```

Combining Model and Optimizer State

You can save both the model and optimizer state in a single file using a dictionary.

```
std::string checkpointPath = "checkpoint.bin";
std::unordered_map<std::string, fl::Variable> checkpoint = {
    {"model", model.params()},
    {"optimizer", optimizer.state().params()},
    // Add other state variables if needed
};
fl::save(checkpointPath, checkpoint);
```

Loading Models

If you want to use the saved model for inference or further training, You will need to load the model's parameters from the file.

For example:

```
#include <flashlight/flashlight.h>
// Initialize the model architecture
ResNetModel model(numClasses);
// Load the model parameters
std::string modelPath = "trained_model.bin";
fl::load(modelPath, model);
```

Here, **fl::load** deserializes the model's parameters from the specified file and loads them into the model.

If continuing training, you may also load the optimizer state as shown below:

```
fl::load(optimizerPath, optimizer);
```

If you saved a combined checkpoint, you can load the components accordingly.

```
std::unordered_map<std::string, fl::Variable> checkpoint;
fl::load(checkpointPath, checkpoint);
model.setParams(checkpoint["model"]);
optimizer.loadStateDict(checkpoint["optimizer"]);
```

Sample Program: Saving and Loading a Trained Model

Let us now go through a complete walk through a practical example of saving and loading our trained ResNet model for inference.

First, let us consider that we have trained the **ResNetModel** on the CIFAR-10 dataset:

```
// After training
std::string modelPath = "resnet_cifar10.bin";
fl::save(modelPath, model);
```

Now in a separate application or at a later time, we can load the model to perform inference. For example:

```
#include <flashlight/flashlight.h>
#include "resnet_model.h"
int main() {
    // Initialize the model architecture
    ResNetModel model(numClasses);
    // Load the model parameters
    std::string modelPath = "resnet_cifar10.bin";
    fl::load(modelPath, model);
    // Set the model to evaluation mode
    model.eval();
    // Load an image for inference
    fl::Tensor image = loadImage("test_image.png"); //
Implement loadImage function
```

```
    image = preprocessImage(image); // Implement preprocessing
steps (e.g., resizing, normalization)
    // Move the image to the appropriate device
    if (fl::cuda::isAvailable()) {
        image = image.to(fl::dtype::f32,
fl::MemoryLocation::CUDA);
    }
    // Create a Variable without gradient tracking
    fl::Variable inputVar(image, /* requiresGrad */ false);
    // Perform inference
    auto output = model.forward(inputVar);
    // Get predicted class
    auto probabilities = output.tensor();
    int predictedClass = fl::argmax(probabilities, /* axis */
0).asScalar<int>();
    std::cout << "Predicted class: " << predictedClass <<
std::endl;
    return 0;
}
```

Now here it is important to ensure the input image matches the expected format (size, normalization). If this is confirmed, then you can forward the input through the model to get the desired predictions.

Implementing 'loadImage' and 'preprocessImage' Functions

Now here, since the Flashlight may not have built-in image loading functions, you can use an external library such as OpenCV which is considered to be the best choice for such applications.

```
#include <opencv2/opencv.hpp>
fl::Tensor loadImage(const std::string& imagePath) {
    cv::Mat img = cv::imread(imagePath);
    if (img.empty()) {
```

```
        throw std::runtime_error("Failed to load image: " +
imagePath);
    }
    cv::cvtColor(img, img, cv::COLOR_BGR2RGB); // Convert to
RGB
    img.convertTo(img, CV_32FC3, 1.0 / 255.0); // Normalize
pixel values to [0, 1]
    // Convert to Flashlight tensor
    int height = img.rows;
    int width = img.cols;
    int channels = img.channels();
    fl::Tensor tensor = fl::Tensor::fromBuffer({channels,
height, width}, img.ptr<float>(), fl::MemoryLocation::Host);
    return tensor;
}
```

After this, adjust the image to match the model's expected input size and you may proceed to perform any necessary normalization, only if needed strictly.

```
fl::Tensor preprocessImage(const fl::Tensor& image) {
    // Resize image if necessary
    fl::Tensor resizedImage = fl::resize(image, 32, 32); //
For CIFAR-10 input size
    // Normalize the image (optional)
    // Subtract mean and divide by standard deviation if used
during training
    return resizedImage;
}
```

Saving and Loading in Checkpoints

Now when training models over long periods, it's common to save checkpoints periodically. Folllwing is the best example to do it:

```
for (int epoch = 1; epoch <= numEpochs; ++epoch) {
```

```
    // Training loop
    // ...
    // Save checkpoint every few epochs
    if (epoch % checkpointInterval == 0) {
        std::string checkpointPath = "checkpoint_epoch_" +
std::to_string(epoch) + ".bin";
        fl::save(checkpointPath, model);
    }
}
```

What's great about this is that you can pick up right where you left off if you have to take a break, and you can even analyze how your model performs at different training stages. I can serialize our trained models effectively, which means we can deploy them for inference, share them with others, or resume training as needed.

Real-time Inference

If you want to be able to make predictions in real time, you need to make sure your application can process the data and generate predictions quickly. This is really important for things like video analysis, real-time monitoring systems, or interactive user interfaces. Here, we're going to improve our C++ application so it can perform real-time inference using our trained model.

There are three main types of common real-time data sources:

- Live video streams from webcams or IP cameras
- Sensor data from IoT devices or other sensors
- User input, which could be real-time data from people using the system

For this example, we will focus on processing frames from a live webcam feed.

Setting up Real-time Data Acquisition

To begin with, we use OpenCV to capture video from a webcam.

```
#include <opencv2/opencv.hpp>
// In your main function
cv::VideoCapture cap(0); // 0 is the default camera
```

```
if (!cap.isOpened()) {
    std::cerr << "Error: Could not open camera." << std::endl;
    return 1;
}
```

Next, we set up a loop to read frames from the camera.

```
while (true) {
    cv::Mat frame;
    cap >> frame; // Capture a new frame
    if (frame.empty()) {
        std::cerr << "Error: Blank frame grabbed." <<
std::endl;
        break;
    }
    // Process the frame
    // ...
    // Display the frame
    cv::imshow("Webcam Feed", frame);
    // Break the loop on key press
    if (cv::waitKey(1) >= 0) {
        break;
    }
}
```

Integrating Inference into Loop

We then resize and normalize the frame to match the model's input requirements.

```
// Resize the frame to 32x32
cv::Mat resizedFrame;
cv::resize(frame, resizedFrame, cv::Size(32, 32));
// Convert to RGB
```

```
cv::cvtColor(resizedFrame, resizedFrame, cv::COLOR_BGR2RGB);
// Normalize pixel values
resizedFrame.convertTo(resizedFrame, CV_32FC3, 1.0 / 255.0);
// Convert to Flashlight tensor
std::vector<int> dims = {resizedFrame.channels(),
resizedFrame.rows, resizedFrame.cols};
std::vector<float> frameData(resizedFrame.total() *
resizedFrame.channels());
std::memcpy(frameData.data(), resizedFrame.data,
resizedFrame.total() * resizedFrame.channels() *
sizeof(float));
fl::Tensor inputTensor = fl::Tensor::fromVector(dims,
frameData);
// Add batch dimension
inputTensor = fl::reshape(inputTensor, {inputTensor.dim(0),
inputTensor.dim(1), inputTensor.dim(2), 1});
// Move to appropriate device
if (fl::cuda::isAvailable()) {
    inputTensor = inputTensor.to(fl::dtype::f32,
fl::MemoryLocation::CUDA);
}
fl::Variable inputVar(inputTensor, /* requiresGrad */ false);
```

Next thing we do is to perform inference as below:

```
auto output = model.forward(inputVar);
// Get predicted class
auto probabilities = output.tensor();
int predictedClass = fl::argmax(probabilities, /* axis */
0).asScalar<int>();
// Optional: Get confidence scores
float confidence =
probabilities(predictedClass).asScalar<float>();
```

Then we overlay the prediction on the video feed.

```
// Map class index to label
std::string label = classLabels[predictedClass];
// Overlay label on the frame
cv::putText(frame, label, cv::Point(10, 30),
            cv::FONT_HERSHEY_SIMPLEX, 1.0, cv::Scalar(0, 255,
0), 2);
```

Implementing Multi-threading

Now here, we make use of eparate threads for capturing frames and processing them separately as below.

- Include Thread Libraries

```
#include <thread>
#include <queue>
#include <mutex>
#include <condition_variable>
```

- Setup a Thread-safe Queue

```
std::queue<cv::Mat> frameQueue;
std::mutex queueMutex;
std::condition_variable queueCondVar;
```

- Frame the Capture Thread

```
void captureFrames(cv::VideoCapture& cap) {
    while (true) {
        cv::Mat frame;
        cap >> frame;
        if (frame.empty()) break;
        {
            std::lock_guard<std::mutex> lock(queueMutex);
```

```
            frameQueue.push(frame);
        }
        queueCondVar.notify_one();
        // Optionally limit the queue size
    }
}
```

- Inference Thread

```
void processFrames() {
    while (true) {
        cv::Mat frame;
        {
            std::unique_lock<std::mutex> lock(queueMutex);
            queueCondVar.wait(lock, [] { return
!frameQueue.empty(); });
            frame = frameQueue.front();
            frameQueue.pop();
        }
        // Preprocess and perform inference
        // ...
        // Display or handle the result
        // ...
    }
}
```

- Starting Threads

```
std::thread captureThread(captureFrames, std::ref(cap));
std::thread inferenceThread(processFrames);
// Join threads before exiting
captureThread.join();
```

```
inferenceThread.join();
```

Next we update the display with predictions.

```
// In the main thread or a separate display thread
while (true) {
    // Display the frame with overlaid predictions
    cv::imshow("Webcam Feed", frameWithOverlay);
    if (cv::waitKey(1) >= 0) {
        break;
    }
}
```

If you combine real-time data collection and analysis with your application, you can create interactive and responsive systems that use the power of neural networks.

Summary

To summarize, we progressed from model development to deployment and integration. We began by learning how to save and load models using the Flashlight library to ensure that our trained neural networks could be serialized and reused effectively. This included handling model parameters, optimizer states, and ensuring consistency between saved and loaded architectures.

We then focused on loading the model, preprocessing inputs, performing inference, and handling outputs. On top of that, we implemented real-time inferencing functionality, which allows our application to make timely forecasts using live data sources such as webcam feeds. And, we also addressed performance considerations and optimized our inference code, improving speed and resource utilization to meet the demands of real-time environments.

CHAPTER 9: PARALLELISM AND PERFORMANCE SCALING

Chapter Overview

In our last and final chapter, we explore techniques for improving the performance and scalability of our machine learning applications through parallelism. We will explore the use of GPU acceleration to take advantage of the processing power of modern GPUs to significantly speed up training and inference. Next, we will discuss multi-threading for ML and learn how to effectively manage concurrent tasks to optimize resource utilization.

We will also look at efficient memory management, which is critical for handling large data sets and models without draining system resources. This includes strategies for allocating memory, moving data, and avoiding memory leaks. When you finish this chapter, You will understand how to scale your machine learning applications to improve performance and efficiency, and You will be ready to tackle complex real-life challenges.

Utilizing GPU Acceleration

The computational demands of machine learning tasks increase significantly as models become more complex and datasets grow in size. Due to their ability to efficiently perform parallel computations, graphics processing units (GPUs) have become essential accelerators for deep learning. GPUs excel at parallel execution, with massive architectures consisting of thousands of small cores working simultaneously. Their Single Instruction, Multiple Data (SIMD) structure is particularly suited to the computational patterns of neural networks. By relying on CUDA, developers can organize computations into threads, blocks, and grids. These concepts map well to the hierarchical structure of GPU hardware, ensuring efficient use of resources. The memory considerations are also critical because GPUs provide different levels of memory, such as global, shared, register, and cache, each with different speeds and accessibility. Further performance is achieved by minimizing data transfers between the CPU (host) and GPU (device), and asynchronous operations can reduce latency.

With Flashlight, enabling GPU acceleration involves ensuring that the necessary drivers and libraries, such as CUDA and cuDNN, are installed. When building Flashlight from source, specifying **-DFLASHLIGHT_BACKEND=CUDA** allows the library to incorporate CUDA support. Within the code, checking for GPU availability with if **fl::cuda::isAvailable()** determines whether to proceed on the GPU or CPU. Automatic device management in Flashlight simplifies the process of placing tensors and computations on the GPU.

For example, think of creating a tensor and moving it to the GPU. You may see below:

```
fl::Tensor tensor = fl::rand({1000, 1000});
if (fl::cuda::isAvailable()) {
    tensor = tensor.to(fl::dtype::f32,
fl::MemoryLocation::CUDA);
```

```
}
```

The integration of GPUs into existing code requires the adaptation of data loading and inference routines. For data loading, once a batch of inputs and targets is retrieved, both can be moved to the GPU memory location before constructing variables and performing forward passes. The same principle applies during inference: both the model and the input data should be moved to the GPU, if available, to ensure that the computations run on the GPU's parallel hardware.

If you could see, a call to **fl::cuda::deviceSynchronize()** can be used to synchronize GPU operations as needed. The optimizations also include selecting appropriate data types, such as **fl::dtype::f16** for half-precision, which can speed up computations on supported GPUs. The adjustment of batch sizes to better fit the GPU memory and the use of profiling tools such as NVIDIA Nsight Systems or **nvprof** to identify bottlenecks and guide further optimization of kernel execution and memory transfers. Here, an updated training loop that incorporates GPU acceleration might first ensure that the model is placed on the GPU if available, then move each batch to the GPU and proceed with the standard forward, loss, backward, and update steps. Such changes often result in significant reductions in epoch duration and improved resource utilization, allowing more complex models and larger datasets to be effectively trained.

Multi-threading for ML

C++ provides various options for multi-threading, ranging from the standard library's **<thread>** facilities to more advanced solutions like Intel Threading Building Blocks, OpenMP, and Boost.Thread. The standard library's threading support is often sufficient to parallelize data loading and preprocessing without introducing external dependencies. Furthermore, the Flashlight library integrates well with multi-threaded data pipelines by offering prefetched datasets. This feature simplifies the task of running data loading and preprocessing steps in the background, allowing the main training loop to focus on computations.

Consider the current approach, where data is loaded and processed sequentially in the main training loop. This setup can lead to underutilization of CPU cores since they remain idle while waiting for data to be ready. The goal is to implement a data loader that works in parallel with model training. Below is a quick sample program to integrate multi-threaded data loading into the training pipeline using Flashlight:

```
// Create the base dataset
auto trainDataset =
std::make_shared<CIFAR10Dataset>(trainData, true);


// Apply batching to the dataset
```

```
auto trainBatchDataset = std::make_shared<fl::BatchDataset>(
    trainDataset, batchSize);

// Apply prefetching with multiple threads
int prefetchThreads = 4; // Number of threads used for
prefetching
auto trainPrefetchDataset =
std::make_shared<fl::PrefetchDataset>(
    trainBatchDataset, prefetchThreads);

// Use the prefetch dataset in the training loop
for (auto& batch : *trainPrefetchDataset) {
    // Training code, such as moving data to GPU and
performing
    // forward pass, loss computation, backward pass, and
optimization
    // ...
}
```

In the above sample program, multiple threads load and preprocess data batches in the background. While the GPU processes one batch, the next one is already being prepared. This keeps the hardware working at all times, improving overall throughput. The **prefetchThreads** variable controls how many threads will run concurrently, however finding the right number requires experimentation to balance CPU load and memory usage.

Implementing Custom Multi-threading

If you need more control, you can implement your own threading mechanism. For this, we first define a thread-safe queue:

```
#include <queue>
#include <mutex>
#include <condition_variable>
template <typename T>
class ThreadSafeQueue {
```

```
public:
    void push(const T& item);
    bool tryPop(T& item);
    // ...
private:
    std::queue<T> queue_;
    std::mutex mutex_;
    std::condition_variable condVar_;
};
```

Next, we create a thread that continuously loads and preprocesses data, pushing it into the queue.

```
void dataLoaderThread(ThreadSafeQueue<BatchType>& queue,
Dataset& dataset) {
    for (auto& data : dataset) {
        // Preprocess data
        // ...
        // Push data into the queue
        queue.push(data);
    }
}
```

Within the main thread, we start to consume data from the queue.

```
BatchType batch;
while (queue.tryPop(batch)) {
    // Training code using batch
    // ...
}
```

Here, we need to take care of that threads are properly synchronized using mutexes and condition variables. And, also some management measures to avoid resource leaks.

Implementing Multi-Threaded Preprocessing

If preprocessing is computationally intensive, you can parallelize it. For example, let us try out using OpenMP:

```
#include <omp.h>
void preprocessBatch(std::vector<DataType>& batch) {
    #pragma omp parallel for
    for (size_t i = 0; i < batch.size(); ++i) {
        // Preprocess each data sample
        batch[i] = preprocess(batch[i]);
    }
}
```

Be certain that operations within the loop are thread-safe. At compile time, you need to enable OpenMP support using the **-fopenmp** flag. Through the use of threading libraries and Flashlight's built-in capabilities, we can make better use of system resources, reduce training time, and handle larger workloads.

Efficient Memory Management

Inefficient memory usage can lead to excessive memory consumption, slow performance, or even crashes due to out-of-memory errors. Here, we will discuss various memory optimization techniques in C++ that can help manage resources effectively. We will also provide practical examples to illustrate how to implement these techniques in our project.

Memory Optimization Techniques

When dealing with large models and datasets in machine learning applications, efficient memory management is imperative. Thoughtful consideration of data structures, allocation patterns, and resource usage can significantly improve performance and stability. One basic approach is to use smart pointers such as **std::unique_ptr** and **std::shared_ptr**. These pointers automatically handle memory allocation and deallocation, reducing the risk of memory leaks and ensuring that objects are properly discarded when no longer needed. Similarly, important is memory pooling, where a large block of memory is preallocated and subsequent allocations occur within that block. This pre-allocation of memory allows applications to minimize the overhead of frequently creating and destroying memory resources. In addition, the implementation of custom allocators can further tailor allocation strategies to the specific needs of an application.

The choice of efficient data structures is another key factor in memory optimization. The use of containers such as **std::vector** instead of std::list can have a positive impact on memory efficiency, especially when random access is required. Similarly, avoiding unnecessary data copies through references or move semantics helps avoid wasted memory and improves overall throughput.

Memory mapping is another effective technique. With the use of memory-mapped files, applications can access only the required segments of large files on demand, rather than loading entire files into memory at once. Similarly, lazy loading and data streaming approaches ensure that data is loaded only when it is needed, resulting in a smaller memory footprint. In addition, batch data processing helps you handle large data sets without exceeding memory limits by loading and processing smaller chunks of data in a more manageable and resource-efficient manner.

By combining these techniques - ranging from smart pointers and memory pooling to efficient data structures, memory mapping, batch processing, and GPU-focused optimizations - developers can build robust machine learning pipelines that can handle large models and data sets with greater efficiency, stability, and performance.

Implementing Smart Pointers in the Dataset Class

We will implement smart pointers in our project to manage dynamically allocated objects automatically. Suppose we're managing a custom dataset class that loads data samples dynamically. So here, we will use **std::unique_ptr** to manage the memory of these samples.

- Define Dataset Class

```
// custom_dataset.h
#ifndef CUSTOM_DATASET_H
#define CUSTOM_DATASET_H
#include <flashlight/flashlight.h>
#include <memory>
#include <vector>
class CustomDataset : public fl::Dataset {
public:
    CustomDataset(const std::string& dataPath);
    ~CustomDataset() override = default;
    // Override size and get functions
    int64_t size() const override;
    std::vector<fl::Tensor> get(const int64_t idx) const
override;
private:
```

```
    std::vector<std::unique_ptr<SampleType>> dataSamples_;
};
#endif // CUSTOM_DATASET_H
```

- Implement Constructor and Data Loading

```
// custom_dataset.cpp
#include "custom_dataset.h"
CustomDataset::CustomDataset(const std::string& dataPath) {
    // Load data samples
    for (const auto& file : listFiles(dataPath)) {
        auto sample = std::make_unique<SampleType>();
        // Load the sample data
        sample->loadFromFile(file);
        // Store the sample using unique_ptr
        dataSamples_.emplace_back(std::move(sample));
    }
}
int64_t CustomDataset::size() const {
    return dataSamples_.size();
}
std::vector<fl::Tensor> CustomDataset::get(const int64_t idx)
const {
    // Access the sample using unique_ptr
    const auto& sample = dataSamples_[idx];
    // Return the data as tensors
    return {sample->inputTensor, sample->targetTensor};
}
```

If you use **std::unique_ptr<SampleType>** in this case, you can rest easy knowing that any memory allocated for **SampleType** instances will be taken care of for you. The **unique_ptr** handles deleting the object when it goes out of scope, so you don't have to worry about explicitly deallocating memory. When you call **std::move(sample)** before inserting the object into the vector, the **unique_ptr** within the container takes ownership of the sample's memory. This makes memory management easier and prevents memory leaks, because each **SampleType** object is guaranteed to be properly deallocated when it's no longer needed.

Optimizing GPU Memory Usage

Mixed Precision Traning

Consider a scenario where GPU memory is limited, and it becomes essential to ensure that the model fits comfortably into the available space. Here, one effective strategy is to implement mixed precision training, where half-precision (16-bit floating-point) computations are used instead of full 32-bit floating-point operations.

```
// Enable mixed precision
fl::setGlobalFloatType(fl::dtype::f16);
// Training code remains the same
```

By employing half-precision, the model's memory footprint decreases, allowing more extensive models or larger batch sizes to be processed without exceeding memory limits. It is important to note that mixed precision training requires hardware support, typically found in NVIDIA GPUs with compute capability 7.0 or higher. When these prerequisites are met, mixed precision training can deliver substantial memory savings and often improves computational speed, providing a more resource-efficient training process.

Gradient Accumulation

In situations where GPU memory is limited, gradient accumulation provides a practical approach to training models without overextending available resources. Instead of processing a large batch all at once, we reduce the batch size to smaller, memory-friendly increments. This means the model trains on multiple smaller batches, each time computing gradients but not immediately updating the weights. Instead, these gradients are accumulated over several iterations. Once enough small batches have been processed, a single weight update is performed based on the aggregated gradients.

See the following example:

```
int accumulationSteps = 4; // Number of small batches to
accumulate
int adjustedBatchSize = batchSize / accumulationSteps;
for (int epoch = 1; epoch <= numEpochs; ++epoch) {
    model.train();
```

```
    float trainLoss = 0.0;
    int step = 0;
    for (auto& batch : *trainDataLoader) {
        // ... (load and preprocess data)
        // Forward pass
        auto outputs = model.forward(inputVar);
        // Compute loss
        auto loss = criterion(outputs, targetVar);
        // Backward pass
        loss.backward();
        // Accumulate gradients
        if ((step + 1) % accumulationSteps == 0) {
            // Update weights
            optimizer.step();
            optimizer.zeroGrad();
        }
        trainLoss += loss.scalar<float>();
        step++;
    }
}
```

In the above example, the idea is that you can effectively train with an effective larger batch size, even when memory constraints prevent loading all those samples at the same time. This ensures that the model can still make stable updates and progress in optimization.

Release Unused Tensors

It's important to free up resources on the GPU when You are done with a particular tensor. Freeing up unused tensors frees up memory that can then be used for other calculations. You can tell the system to give that memory back to the pool by explicitly clearing the tensors, for example by calling **fl::Tensor::unlock()** or simply reassigning a tensor variable to a new value. This helps you to use memory efficiently, prevents bottlenecks and makes sure that the GPU is ready for the next task without wasting memory.

See the following example:

```
// After using a tensor
inputTensor = fl::Tensor(); // Releases the tensor's memory
```

It's important to manage memory efficiently if you want your machine learning applications to be scalable and robust. There are a few techniques we can use, such as smart pointers, optimizing data structures, and managing GPU memory carefully. These techniques help us handle large models and datasets effectively, prevent memory leaks, reduce resource consumption, and improve the performance of our applications overall.

Summary

To summarize, we focused on improving the performance and scalability of machine learning applications by parallelizing and using efficient resources. We began by exploring GPU acceleration, discussing key concepts such as CUDA programming, memory hierarchy, and data transfer overhead. We demonstrated how GPUs can be used to achieve significant speedups in training and inference by integrating GPU support into our C++ projects using the Flashlight library. Techniques such as offloading computations to the GPU, adjusting batch sizes, and taking advantage of mixed precision were all used to optimize performance.

We then looked at multi-threading, showing how concurrent execution can improve the efficiency of data loading and preprocessing. Using the threading facilities, we implemented multi-threaded data loaders to reduce idle time and improve throughput. We also discussed efficient memory management strategies such as using smart pointers, memory pooling, and avoiding unnecessary data copies to effectively handle large models and datasets. This provided us with practical skills to scale machine learning applications effectively.

Index

S

T

W

Epilogue

As we conclude this book, I am confident that the knowledge and skills you have acquired will serve as a robust foundation for the projects you will undertake in the future. Once you have a solid understanding of C++ and its powerful data structures and libraries, you will be ready to take on any challenge. The field of machine learning is vast and constantly evolving. You are ready to take on whatever challenges come your way.

You had come across various practical techniques and strategies in this book, ranging from the implementation of advanced neural networks to the optimization of performance with GPU acceleration, will serve as building blocks for your future innovations. You must incorporate these learnings into your work, and you will undoubtedly succeed in developing high-performing machine learning applications that take advantage of the speed and efficiency of C++.

Keep exploring, experimenting, and pushing the boundaries of what is possible. You can do this. You know you have the tools and the know-how to make a big impact in the field.

--- Anais Sutherland

Thank You

www.ingramcontent.com/pod-product-compliance
Lightning Source LLC
Chambersburg PA
CBHW080214170726
48282CB00030B/1117
* 9 7 8 8 1 9 7 9 5 0 4 8 3 *